Editorial Project Manager
Lorin E. Klistoff, M.A

Editor-in-Chief
Sharon Coan, M.S. Ed.

Illustrator
Ken Tunell

Cover Artist
Barb Lorseyedi

Art Coordinator
Kevin Barnes

Art Director
CJae Froshay

Imaging
James Edward Grace

Product Manager
Phil Garcia

Publisher
Mary D. Smith, M.S. Ed.

Author

Mary Tucker

Teacher Created Resources, Inc.
6421 Industry Way
Westminster, CA 92683
www.teachercreated.com
ISBN-0-7439-7029-2
©2003 Teacher Created Resources, Inc.
Reprinted, 2005
Made in U.S.A.

Table of Contents

Introduction

Character building has had a resurgence of popularity in the last decade or so. Even in public schools where absolutely nothing "religious" is to be taught, there are a variety of methods being used to teach children love, kindness, patience, and generally how to get along with others. Of course, trying to teach a child positive character traits without introducing that child to the only One who can change his or her heart is somewhat futile. How fortunate we are that the Bible, God's Word, tells us exactly how we can instill character in our children—by leading them to receive Jesus as their Savior. When they give their lives to Him, the Holy Spirit comes to live in them and begins to grow godly character traits in them.

When we teach children about the fruit of the Spirit, we latch onto the idea of fruit—apples, oranges, grapes—as a way to simplify and illustrate the idea. However, we need to go beyond the illustration of mixed fruit in a bowl to the truths behind the illustration. The activities in this book will help children understand the fruit of the Spirit—where it comes from, how they can demonstrate it in their everyday lives, and how Jesus set an example for demonstrating the fruit of the Spirit in His relationships with His Father and with other people. Activities include puzzles, coded messages, mini-books, rhymes, songs, acrostics, crafts, object lessons, and various other creative teaching ideas.

Each lesson begins with a Bible story of a person who demonstrated the fruit of the Spirit in his or her life. The stories are presented in a variety of creative ways to capture children's attention and hold it. The story is followed by a memory verse and a bulletin board idea. Each lesson includes 6–7 pages of Bible activities to involve children in discovering for themselves the importance of each fruit mentioned in Galatians 5:22–23. The lessons are based on the New International Version Bible. An answer key is provided at the back of the book.

As you teach children about the fruit of the Spirit, make sure to give them opportunities to practice what they learn. If possible, schedule some times outside class for taking the children to a nursing home to visit with the residents and share what they are learning. Take a few of your children to visit a sick class member or someone else in your church who would appreciate a visit. Encourage each child to look for ways at home to practice patience and gentleness with younger siblings. Hold them accountable by asking them to report their experiences of living out the fruit of the Spirit at home, school, and wherever they go.

You cannot emphasize enough the role of the Holy Spirit in helping children practice the fruit of the Spirit. They know the right thing to do and will probably do it when parents or teachers are around to encourage them. But what happens when they are with their peers and temptation comes? Make sure they understand that they can always count on the Holy Spirit to help them do the right thing. Be sure to pray for each of your students by name as they study these lessons, that the Holy Spirit will become real to them and that they will give control of their lives to Him.

Bible Story (Ruth)

Directions: Have students act out this familiar story in the book of Ruth. You will need to assign parts: a Narrator, Naomi, Ruth, Orpah, Boaz, harvest foreman, and field workers. Make copies and involve the class.

Narrator: There was a famine in the land of Judah which meant that people were starving. Some moved to other lands where they could grow enough food to eat. A Jewish woman named Naomi moved with her husband and two sons to Moab. While they were living there, her sons married women from that land. Naomi's husband died; then her two sons died. She was left in a strange land with her two daughters-in-law. When Naomi heard that the famine in Judah was over, she decided to go back home.

Naomi: *(Sadly, with arms around Ruth and Orpah)* I will go back to my homeland, but you two must stay here with your own people, and may God bless you and find you new husbands.

Orpah: *(Crying)* But we want to go with you!

Ruth: *(Crying)* We will go to Judah too!

Naomi: No, no, you must stay here, but I will miss you.

Orpah: *(Hugs Naomi and walks away.)*

Ruth: Don't try to talk me into staying here. I am going with you to Judah. I love you. I will serve your God and your people will be my people.

Naomi: Very well then, let's go.

Narrator: When they got to Bethlehem, Naomi's hometown, everyone was excited to see her again. They settled down and Naomi began trying to figure out how she and Ruth would live.

Ruth: The barley harvest has just started. Let me go and pick up leftover barley in the fields so we'll have something to eat!

Naomi: Go ahead.

Ruth: *(Follows other field workers around, picking up barley stalks from the ground.)*

Boaz: *(With the harvest foreman, watching Ruth work)* Who is that young woman?

Foreman: That's Ruth, Naomi's daughter-in-law from Moab. She asked if she could pick up the leftover barley and I told her she could, since she and Naomi are both widows with no one to care for them. She's worked hard since this morning.

Boaz: *(To Ruth)* You're welcome to stay here in my field to get as much barley as you need. No one will bother you and there's water for you to drink.

Ruth: *(To Boaz)* Why are you being so kind to me?

Boaz: *(To Ruth)* I've heard about the way you're caring for your mother-in-law. May the Lord reward you for your goodness.

Narrator: When a meal was served, Boaz encouraged Ruth to eat with his workers. *(Ruth and other workers sit and eat.)* He told his men to leave extra barley for Ruth to pick up.

Naomi: *(To Ruth as she hands her a bag of barley)* Wonderful! Where did you get all this?

Ruth: In a field that belongs to a man named Boaz.

Naomi: What? Why, Boaz is a relative of my husband's! God bless him! You stay in his field; he will look out for you.

Narrator: Ruth kept working in the field of Boaz, and they fell in love and got married. Naomi was thrilled at what the Lord had done, especially when Ruth's first child was born!

Naomi: *(Talking to Ruth's baby as she holds him in her arms)* Obed, my child, I lost two sons, but now God has given you to me. And your mother is better to me than seven sons! I am an old woman, but I feel young again! Praise God for His goodness!

Narrator: God had blessed Naomi even more than she knew, for Obed grew up to become the grandfather of David, the greatest king Israel ever had.

Verse/Bulletin Board

Verse

"Dear friends, let us love one another, for love comes from God." (1 John 4:7a)

Talk about the love that was shown in the story of Ruth and Naomi. Ruth loved her mother-in-law so much she refused to leave her and worked hard to provide for her. God rewarded her unselfish love by giving her a husband and a son to love her.

Have each student cut out a large heart shape and print the memory verse on it. On one side, they should print "Dear friends, let us love one another," and on the other side "for loves comes from God." Choose a student to stand in front and hold up the heart turning it at the appropriate time while the others repeat the verse. Do this several times until students have memorized the verse.

Bulletin Board: "Love"

1. Cover the board with red paper.

2. Print the caption on a large red paper heart with a larger white heart behind it.

3. Mount the large hearts at the center of the board.

4. Cut various sizes of hearts from white and pink paper. Print words or phrases from 1 Corinthians 13 to describe love on them.

5. Scatter the hearts around the center hearts.

6. Read all of 1 Corinthians 13 together. Discuss each description of love to make sure everyone understands it. Read Galatians 5:22 to remind students that this kind of love comes from God. It isn't something we can do on our own; we must rely on the Holy Spirit to give us God's love. Have students brainstorm practical ways they can show this kind of love in their everyday lives at home, at school, and wherever they are.

Action Song

Directions: Have students sing this song as they do the actions.

(Tune: "Jump Down, Turn Around, Pick a Bail of Cotton")

Bend down, turn around,

(Bend from the waist and turn around.)

Pick up lots of barley.

(Pretend to scoop up barley with right arm.)

Bend down, turn around,

(Bend from the waist and turn around.)

Pick it up this way.

(Pretend to carry a heavy load.)

Bend down, turn around,

(Bend from the waist and turn around.)

Pick up lots of barley.

(Pretend to scoop up barley with left arm.)

You know the Lord is watchin'

(Point toward heaven.)

And He's blessin' you today.

(Hold both hands over your head and sway.)

Stand up, turn around,

(Stand up tall and turn around.)

Go and help somebody.

(Grab someone's hand.)

Stand up, turn around,

(Stand up tall and turn around.)

Give your love away.

(Put hand on heart, then hold your hand out.)

Stand up, turn around,

(Stand up tall and turn around.)

Go and help somebody.

(Grab someone's hand.)

You know the Lord is watchin'

(Point toward heaven.)

And He's blessin' you today.

(Hold both hands over your head and sway.)

Directions: The Bible tells us that we love because God first loved us. (1 John 4:19) He is our example of how to love. Look up the Bible verses to find the words to complete the sentences about God's love. Then find those same words in the puzzle and circle them.

1. God has _____ out his love into our hearts by the Holy Spirit, whom he has given us. (Romans 5:5)

2. For the Lord is good and his love endures _____. (Psalm 100:5)

3. Though the mountains be shaken and the hills be removed, yet my _____ love for you will not be shaken. (Isaiah 54:10)

4. The Lord appeared to us in the past, saying: "I have loved you with an _____ love; I have drawn you with loving-kindness." (Jeremiah 31:3)

5. How _____ is the love the Father has lavished on us, that we should be called children of God! (1 John 3:1)

6. How _____ is your unfailing love! (Psalm 36:7)

7. The Lord is slow to anger, _____ in love and forgiving sin and rebellion. (Numbers 14:18)

8. This is how God showed his love among us: He sent his one and only _____ into the world that we might live through him. (1 John 4:9)

V	E	P	R	I	C	E	L	E	S	S
Z	V	A	O	L	F	J	G	N	Z	X
L	E	B	Z	U	O	N	P	D	N	U
Q	R	O	V	V	R	Z	B	D	Z	N
R	L	U	J	K	E	E	Q	W	Z	F
N	A	N	Q	B	V	C	D	L	Q	A
B	S	D	R	Z	E	Z	Q	W	M	I
J	T	I	Z	G	R	E	A	T	R	L
F	I	N	M	Z	R	Z	Q	B	Z	I
G	N	G	S	O	N	Z	Q	K	Y	N
Z	G	L	R	D	B	N	N	Q	R	G

A Hidden Message

Directions: Color every square that has one **X** in it to discover a wonderful message for you from the Bible.

How does this message make you feel?

Everyday Love Booklet

Directions

Follow the directions below to make an Everyday Love Booklet.

1. Copy the envelope pattern below and the booklet from page 10 for each student.

2. Have students cut the booklet pattern on page 10 in half lengthwise, then tape the two long pieces together end to end to make one strip of numbered pages.

3. Read the prayer at the beginning of the booklet. Have students sign their names below the prayer, then write on the small pages specific ways they can show love. Go through all of the pages together. Give the students the option of coloring each page a different color.

4. Show students how to accordion fold the long strip and hold it together with a paper clip.

5. Have students cut out the envelope pattern below and color it or decorate it with small, heart stickers.

6. Show students how to fold along the broken lines to make an envelope.

7. Provide glue or transparent tape for students to secure the tabs.

8. Have students put their fold-up booklets in the envelopes to take home. Encourage them to read their booklets every day as a reminder to share God's love.

EVERYDAY LOVE

How to show love
every day of the week

Everyday Love Booklet

TUESDAY

Children, obey your parents in everything. (Colossians 3:20)

I will show my love for my parents by obeying and helping them this way:

_____
_____
_____

SATURDAY

Love the brotherhood of believers. (1 Peter 2:17)

This is what I will do to show love to other Christians:

_____
_____
_____

MONDAY

Love your enemies and pray for those who persecute you. (Matthew 5:44)

I will pray for these people today and be kind to them even when they're unkind:

_____
_____

FRIDAY

Respect those who work hard among you, who are over you in the Lord . . . Hold them in the highest regard in love. (1 Thessalonians 5:12–13)

I will show God's love to my pastor by doing this:

_____
_____

SUNDAY

Love the Lord your God. (Matthew 22:37)

This is how I will show my love for God today:

_____
_____
_____

THURSDAY

A friend loves at all times. (Proverbs 17:17)

I will love these friends today by telling them about Jesus:

_____
_____

Dear Lord,

Thank You for loving me.

Help me show Your love

in my life every day,

in every way.

_____
(name)

WEDNESDAY

Love your neighbor as yourself. (Romans 13:9)

I will love this neighbor today by doing this:

_____
_____

Magnetic Bookmarks

Materials

- copies of the bookmark patterns on page 12
- crayons or colored markers
- clear adhesive plastic
- scissors
- magnetic tape

GOD'S
LOVE
IS BIG
ENOUGH
TO HOLD
EVERYBODY!

Directions

1. Let each student choose a bookmark to color and cut out.

2. Show how to cover the front and back of the bookmark with clear adhesive plastic.

3. Have students fold their bookmarks in half on the broken lines with the picture on the outside. Rubbing the fold with a finger will make the top of the bookmark as flat as possible.

4. Attach a piece of magnetic tape to both inside bottom edges of each bookmark.

5. To use the bookmark, slip it over a page. The magnets will cling to each other to hold it in place.

6. Let each student make as many bookmarks as time allows.

7. Encourage students to give the bookmarks as gifts to share God's love. Take time to discuss the sayings on each bookmark. You may want to provide envelopes for students to put their bookmarks in with the names of the recipients on them.

Bookmark Patterns

John 3:16

have eternal life.
but shall not perish
whoever believes in him
only Son, that
he gave his one and
the world that
For God so loved

Romans 8:38–39

Lord.
in Christ Jesus our
God that is in
from the love of
able to separate us
all creation, will be
nor anything else in
height nor depth,
powers, neither
nor any
the future,
the present nor
nor demons, neither
life, neither angels
Neither death nor

I LoVe You

John 15:9

loved you.
loved me, so have I
As the Father has

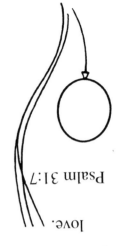

Psalm 31:7

love.
rejoice in your
I will be glad and

GOD'S

LOVE

IS BIG

ENOUGH

TO HOLD

EVERYBODY!

Who or what can make God stop loving you?

Nothing

Nobody

No way

God's love is forever!

I love you, just as you are.

A MESSAGE TO YOU FROM JESUS

CELEBRATE GOD'S LOVE!

12

Bible Story (Nehemiah)

Directions: Before you tell the story of Nehemiah rebuilding the wall (Nehemiah 2–4; 6; 8), draw a stone wall on the board. As you describe the condition of the wall when Nehemiah saw it, erase sections of the wall. Redraw those sections a little at a time as you tell how Nehemiah and the people rebuilt it. Use a few simple props and actions to tell the rest of the story.

Nehemiah was a Jewish man who had never seen his homeland. He had been born in a strange land because his parents had been brought captive to the land when their homeland was conquered. Nehemiah became the cupbearer to the king, the most powerful man in the land. Nehemiah tasted all food and drink to make sure it wasn't poisoned before it was served to the king. *(Hold up a fancy glass or cup and pretend to drink from it.)* It was a dangerous job, but it was important.

One day Nehemiah heard some very bad news: the wall around the city of Jerusalem in his homeland was broken down *(erase sections of the wall)* and its gates had been burned with fire. Though he had never been to the city, Nehemiah cried and didn't eat. Jerusalem was such an important city to the Jewish people, he couldn't stand the thought of it being in ruins, so Nehemiah prayed. *(Fold your hands and bow your head.)* He asked God to help him talk to the king and get permission to go to Jerusalem and rebuild the wall.

The next time Nehemiah took wine to the king it was with a sad look on his face. *(Look sad)* Nehemiah had always been a joyful person, so the king said to him, "Why does your face look so sad when you are not ill? This can be nothing but sadness of the heart." This was exactly the chance Nehemiah was hoping for!

"I am sad because the city where my fathers are buried is in ruins and its gates have been destroyed by fire!" Nehemiah said. When the king asked him what he wanted, Nehemiah asked for permission to travel to the city of Jerusalem to rebuild the wall. The king agreed and provided his cup bearer with letters that would assure his safe conduct to the city and provide timber for rebuilding the wall and its gates. He even sent soldiers along for protection. Nehemiah was filled with joy at the way God had answered his prayer.

When Nehemiah finally got to Jerusalem, he went to look at the wall at night because he didn't want anyone to know why he was there yet. After he saw for himself the terrible condition of the wall, Nehemiah met with some of the priests and officials in the city.

"Come, let us rebuild the wall of Jerusalem, and we will no longer be in disgrace!" he said. Then he explained how God had helped him. They all agreed to begin the work immediately. When outsiders ridiculed Nehemiah and tried to stop him, he answered, "The God of heaven will give us success."

The people worked hard. First, they repaired the gates. *(Draw back parts of the wall.)* Then everyone—city officials, priests, merchants, artists—worked on rebuilding the part of the wall closest to their home. The disagreeable outsiders got angry when they saw the people all working together. They yelled at the workers, trying to discourage them. But it didn't work. The people kept right on working "with all their heart." When the enemy began threatening the workers, Nehemiah assigned guards to watch over the wall and protect the workers day and night.

Finally, Nehemiah had some of the workers bring their swords and spears and bows and arrows. They held a weapon in one hand and rebuilt the wall with the other. Nehemiah joyfully told them, "Don't be afraid of them. Remember the Lord, who is great and awesome." And the rebuilding of the wall went on. *(Keep drawing the missing parts of the wall and adding even more stones.)*

It took only 52 days to finish the wall around Jerusalem. Everyone, even the Jews' enemies, realized that the work had been done with the help of God! Ezra the scribe brought out the Book of the Law to read it to the people in the city square. When he opened it, he praised God and all the people lifted their hands and shouted "Amen! Amen!" Then everyone bowed down and worshiped the Lord. For six hours God's Word was read aloud and everyone listened in silence. Then Nehemiah said to the people, "This is a day to rejoice! Go and eat the best food and drink the sweetest drinks and share with others. This day is sacred to the Lord. Do not be sad, for the joy of the Lord is your strength!" All the people went away to eat and drink and celebrate with great joy.

Verse/Bulletin Board

Verse

"... I will rejoice in the LORD, I will be joyful in God my Savior." (Habakkuk 3:18)

Cut stone shapes from grey paper. Write a word or phrase of the memory verse on each one. Be sure to include a stone for the reference also. Lay the the stones in scrambled order on a table or attach them to a wall. Have students see how quickly they can build the wall and put the verse in order. You may want to time students to see who is the fastest.

Have students say the verse together. Then ask them to suggest some reasons they have for rejoicing in the Lord. Sing together the praise chorus, "The Joy of the Lord Is My Strength."

Bulletin Board: "The Joy of the Lord Is Like Sunshine in Our Hearts!"

1. Take an instant photo of each of your students smiling or laughing. To make sure their expressions are for real, let other students tell them jokes or make funny faces as they are posing.

2. Cover the board with blue paper.

3. Print the caption on the background paper with black marker or cut letters for it from yellow paper and mount them across the top of the board.

4. Print the Bible verses on a yellow strip and attach it at the bottom of the board.

5. Let students draw and cut out yellow sun shapes and glue their photos to them.

6. Scatter the photos all over the board.

The Joy of the Lord Is Like Sunshine in Our Hearts!

Our mouths were filled with laughter, our tongues with songs of joy . . . .
The Lord has done great things for us, and we are filled with joy.
(Psalm 126:2–3)

Psalms of Joy

Directions: Many of the Psalms are about the joy God gives those who trust in Him. Complete the acrostic with the missing words from the Bible verses (NIV), all from the book of Psalms. Write the missing words both in the verses and in the acrostic.

1. Let the righteous rejoice in the Lord and take _____ in him; let all the upright in heart praise him! (Psalm 64:10)

2. You have made known to me the path of life; you will fill me with joy in your presence, with _____ pleasures at your right hand. (Psalm 16:11)

3. Shout for joy to the Lord, all the earth, burst into _____ song with music. (Psalm 98:4)

4. May my lips _____ with praise . . . . (Psalm 119:171a)

5. Praise the Lord, O my soul; all my _____ being praise his holy name. (Psalm 103:1)

6. _____, let us sing for joy to the Lord; let us shout aloud to the Rock of our salvation. (Psalm 95:1)

7. But may all who seek you rejoice and be glad in you; may those who love your salvation always say, "Let God be _____!" (Psalm 70:4)

1. **R** ___ ___ ___ ___ ___

2. **E** ___ ___ ___ ___ ___ ___

3. **J** ___ ___ ___ ___ ___ ___ ___

4. **O** ___ ___ ___ ___ ___ ___ ___ ___

5. **I** ___ ___ ___ ___ ___

6. **C** ___ ___ ___

7. **E** ___ ___ ___ ___ ___ ___ ___

Joy Pyramid

If you want to have lasting joy, you have to know how joy works. The place to go to find that out is the Bible. Here's what God's Word teaches us about how joy works.

1. Give <u>Jesus first</u> place in your life. He is the One who gives you true joy when you give Him your life.

   Jesus said, "Seek first his kingdom and his righteous." (Matthew 6:33a)

2. Put <u>others second</u> in your life. As a Christian, you should be caring for and loving people ahead of your own interests.

   "Do nothing out of selfish ambition or vain conceit, but in humility consider others better than yourselves. Each of you should look not only to your own interests, but also to the interests of others." (Philippians 2:3–4)

3. Put <u>yourself last</u>. You might want to put yourself first, but selfishness only brings temporary happiness or pleasure, not lasting joy.

   "For by the grace given me I say to every one of you: Do not think of yourself more highly than you ought, but rather think of yourself with sober judgment, in accordance with the measure of faith God has given you." (Romans 12:3)

Directions

Make this pyramid reminder of what you have learned.

1. Cut out the pyramid pattern and color each letter section.

2. Fold the pattern on the broken lines.

3. Tape the two ends together to form a pyramid.

4. Read the letter and words on each section in numbered order.

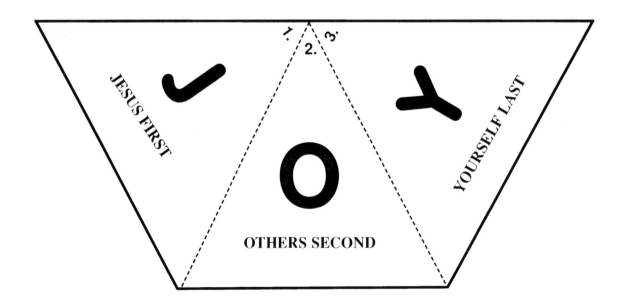

Joyful Wall Plaque

Materials

- colored poster board
- heart patterns (See directions below.)
- cardboard or Styrofoam
- pencils
- colored markers
- scissors
- yarn of various colors
- glue

Directions

1. Before class make large paper heart patterns by folding a sheet of 8 ½" x 11" (22 cm x 28 cm) paper in half, drawing half a heart on it, cutting it out, then unfolding it. Make several.

2. Give each of your students a sheet of poster board about 8 ½" x 11" (22 cm x 28 cm). Have them trace the heart pattern on the poster board and cut it out.

3. Have students draw the word "JOY" in large letters (about 2" [5 cm] tall) on cardboard or Styrofoam and cut them out. (You will need to do this for younger students.)

4. Have them color the letters, then show them how to smear each letter with glue and decorate it with whirls, loops, and twists of colored yarn.

5. Have students use pencils to neatly print on their hearts: "Jesus put JOY in my heart." Have them leave plenty of space to glue their large "JOY" letters on the heart in the middle of this statement.

6. Have them go over their pencil printing with colored markers; then carefully glue down their decorated "JOY" letters on the heart.

7. Show them how to glue a length of colored yarn to the top of the heart for a hanger.

Joy Action Song

Directions: Teach children this joyful song. Sing it slowly at first so they can copy your actions as they sing; then speed it up to a livelier tempo.

I've Got Joy

(Tune: "She'll Be Comin' 'Round the Mountain When She Comes")

I've got joy that Jesus gave me in my heart.

(Clap your hands, then point to your heart.)

I've got joy that Jesus gave me in my heart.

(Clap your hands, then point to your heart.)

I've got joy that Jesus gave me when I asked Him and He saved me.

(Clap your hands, point to heaven, then cross your hands over your heart.)

I've got joy that Jesus gave me in my heart.

(Clap your hands, then point to your heart.)

I've got joy that I just cannot explain.

(Clap your hands, then point to your head.)

I've got joy that I just cannot explain.

(Clap your hands, then point to your head.)

I've got joy I can't explain, but it always will remain.

(Clap your hands, point to your head, then open your arms wide.)

I've got joy that I just cannot explain.

(Clap your hands, then point to your head.)

I've got joy, and you know you can have it too.

(Clap your hands, then point to another person.)

I've got joy, and you know you can have it too.

(Clap your hands, then point to another person.)

Just say, "Jesus, I believe," and His joy you will receive.

(Fold your hands and bow your head; then smile big with your hands framing your mouth.)

I've got joy, and you know you can have it too.

(Clap your hands, then point to another person.)

His Joy

Directions: Did you know that you bring joy to God? Follow the directions to complete the Bible verse. Look up Zephaniah 3:17 to check your work. Cross off every *B*, *K*, and *Q*. Write the remaining letters in order on the lines at the bottom of the page.

H	Q	B	E	K	W	I	Q
K	L	Q	L	Q	K	B	R
E	K	B	K	J	O	Q	K
Q	I	Q	C	Q	B	K	B
E	K	B	O	V	K	Q	E
B	R	K	Q	Q	Y	B	K
O	U	B	K	W	B	Q	I
K	Q	T	B	K	B	H	K
S	B	Q	I	Q	N	K	Q
B	G	K	Q	I	B	N	G

THE LORD YOUR GOD IS WITH YOU, HE IS MIGHTY TO SAVE.
HE WILL TAKE GREAT DELIGHT IN YOU, HE WILL QUIET YOU WITH HIS LOVE,

___ ___   ___ ___ ___ ___

___ ___ ___ ___ ___ ___ ___ ___ ___ ___ ___ ___ ___

___ ___ ___ ___ ___   ___ ___ ___ ___ ___

___ ___ ___ ___ ___ ___ ___ ___ ___ ___ .

Joyful Object Lesson

Materials

- a clear glass of water
- food coloring
- cooking oil
- spoon

Directions

Ask students if they can tell the difference between joy and happiness. Most dictionaries use them interchangeably, as synonyms. But Christians know that there is a real difference between the two. Explain the following to the students:

Joy is a deep-down feeling that we are given by the Holy Spirit. Because it comes from God, it doesn't change when there are changes around us. Joy stays the same even when we are going through trouble or hard times. Inner joy is not affected by outer circumstances. Joy makes it possible to go through difficulty without falling apart or giving up. *(As you talk, pour some food coloring in the glass of water and stir it.)*

True joy is not easily explained to anyone who hasn't experienced it. Peter, describing what Jesus has done for us, said: "Though you have not seen him, you love him; and even though you do not see him now, you believe in him and are filled with an inexpressible and glorious joy." (1 Peter 1:8) Even Peter could not explain the joy the Holy Spirit gives those who love Jesus. Like this food coloring colored this water, joy colors the whole life of the Christian. Joy may surprise you. When you are experiencing trouble or sorrow, the joy of the Spirit will keep you afloat instead of letting you drown in discouragement and sadness.

Happiness, however, is a temporary feeling based on our circumstances. We are happy when life is going well and good things are happening to us. Happiness can be brought on by getting good grades, winning a basketball game, or your mother putting homemade brownies in your lunch. Happiness is a good thing, but it's temporary. *(As you talk, pour some oil into the glass of colored water.)* It's not a deep-down feeling like joy is, but it stays on the surface of our lives just as this oil stays on the surface of the water. Happiness is "here today, gone tomorrow."

Which would you rather have—joy or happiness?

Joy Games

Since some of the following games may be noisy and active, plan to play them outside or in a gym if possible.

Follow the Joyful Leader

Ask students to think about how they express joy. Choose a student to stand in front of the class and demonstrate a favorite way of expressing joy (smiling, laughing, clapping, shouting, jumping up and down, etc.). The other students should follow his or her leading and express their joy the same way. Then choose another student to lead the class in expressing joy in another way. Continue until every student who wants to be involved has a chance to be the leader.

Pass-Along-the-Joy Relay

Divide students into two or three teams, depending on the size of your class. Have each team line up at a starting line. Give the first person on each team a baton made from a cardboard roll from paper towels on which you have printed the word "JOY." At your signal, the first student on each team runs to a previously designated line, then runs back to his or her team and hands the baton to the next team member. That student runs as quickly as possible to the line, then back to pass along the baton to the next runner. To make sure students play fairly (which they sometimes neglect to do in the heat of competition), have an adult or teen helper stationed at the line to which they run. Explain that the runners must touch the hand of that person before running back to the team. Also, make sure the runners getting ready to receive the batons stay behind the starting line until they have the batons in hand.

When the relay is over (you may have to hold it more than once to give each team a chance to win), have students sit down in a circle. Point out that passing along joy to others is obviously not as simple as passing a baton in a race. Ask them to share their ideas about how to pass along the joy Jesus gives. When a student says that telling someone about Jesus is a way to pass the joy along, briefly discuss the plan of salvation. What should we say to explain to someone how to receive Jesus as Savior? End this discussion time by praying, asking God to help each student pass along the joy in his or her heart to help someone else find it too.

Cheers and Songs of Joy

Divide students into small groups of three or four. Challenge each group to compose a cheer or a song about joy and perform it for the rest of the class. As students make their plans, quietly walk around and listen briefly to each group to answer questions and offer help if needed.

Creative Art Contest

Print the following Bible verse on the board or print it on paper and give a copy to each student:

"May the God of hope fill you with all joy and peace as you trust in him, so that you may

overflow with hope by the power of the Holy Spirit." (Romans 15:13)

Provide art materials such as paper, pencils, and crayons or markers. Challenge students to draw pictures to illustrate the Bible verse. When the illustrations are finished, let students hold them up and explain them. Mount them on a wall and let students vote by secret ballot for the favorite one.

Bible Story (Daniel)

Directions: Tell the story of Daniel in the lions' den (based on Daniel 6) by coloring and cutting out the patterns on page 24. Glue the figure of Daniel standing on a craft stick. Glue the figure of Daniel praying on the other side of the stick. Glue the figure of the roaring lions on one side of another craft stick and the lions lying down on the other side. Use these puppets to tell the story of Daniel.

(Hold up Daniel standing.) Daniel was a man filled with God's peace. He didn't worry about what anyone else thought of him; he cared only what God thought. Daniel had come to the land of Babylon as a young captive when the Babylonian King Nebuchadnezzar invaded and conquered his land. He was chosen to be specially trained to serve in the king's palace. From the very beginning, Daniel stood for the Lord rather than go along with everything the ungodly Babylonians suggested. God blessed Daniel by giving him an important job in the government.

Now, Daniel was an old man, still a captive in the land of Babylon, but serving a different king named Darius. The king was so impressed with Daniel's work, he planned to promote him. This made some of the other government officials jealous and they decided to bring charges against Daniel to get him removed from his job. Daniel was such a godly man, they couldn't find one thing he had done wrong! So, they decided to trick King Darius into getting rid of Daniel.

One of the things everyone knew about Daniel was that he loved to pray to God. *(Turn over the puppet to the figure of Daniel praying.)* He prayed at least three times a day in front of windows in his house that faced his homeland. The jealous officials decided to use Daniel's praying as a weapon against him. *(Put down the puppet.)* They spoke to the king, flattering him: "O King Darius, may you live forever! We have all agreed that you should make a decree that anyone who prays to any god or man other than you for the next 30 days shall be thrown to the lions!" The men convinced King Darius to write down the decree and sign it to make it the law of the land. Of course, the king had no idea the men had an evil purpose in mind.

What did Daniel do when he heard of the new law? *(Hold up Daniel praying.)* He went right on praying three times a day as he always had. He bowed down in the usual place, right in front of the windows where anyone could see him. Of course, when the jealous officials saw him praying, they pretended to be

shocked and dismayed. They immediately ran to the king and said, "Daniel is not paying attention to you! He is praying three times a day to his God. What are you going to do about it?" *(Put down the puppet.)*

King Darius didn't want to punish Daniel. He tried all day to find a way to get around the law he had made, but it was no use. He had signed his name to the law and the jealous officials reminded him that he couldn't change it. Finally, the king had Daniel brought to him. "May your God, whom you serve continually, rescue you," he said to Daniel. Then he ordered him thrown into the lions' den. *(Hold up roaring lions.)* A stone was placed over the doorway of the den so no one could try to help Daniel escape. Then the king went back to his palace where he spent a sleepless night, regretting what he had done. What do you think was happening in the lions' den that night? *(Hold up Daniel praying in one hand and the roaring lions in the other.)* While the king was nervously pacing the floor in his palace, Daniel was at peace right in the midst of great danger. Daniel was talking to the Lord and the lions were missing their midnight snack! *(Turn puppet to lions lying down.)*

Early the next morning, as soon as it was light, King Darius hurried to the lions' den and yelled to Daniel, "Has your God been able to rescue you from the lions?" Daniel's calm voice came from the lions' den: "My God shut the mouths of the lions and they have not hurt me!"

The king was overjoyed! *(Put down puppets.)* Daniel was lifted from the lions' den and his accusers were thrown in! *(Hold up roaring lions.)* This time, the Lord did not shut the lions' mouths, and the jealous men were killed. King Darius was so impressed by the way God had kept Daniel safe, he wrote to everyone in the land that they should all honor Daniel's God. "For He is the living God and He endures forever," Darius wrote. *(Put down lions puppet and hold up Daniel standing.)* God continued to bless Daniel, and Daniel continued to pray and serve Him faithfully.

Verse/Bulletin Board

Verse

"I will lie down and sleep in peace, for you alone, O Lord, make me dwell in safety."
(Psalm 4:8)

Help students learn the verse by singing it to a familiar tune such as "God Is So Good" or "Twinkle, Twinkle, Little Star." You will need to squeeze some of the words in near the end, but it can be done without making it difficult to sing. Sing the verse together several times.

Talk about sleeping. Ask students if they ever have trouble sleeping. What kinds of things keep them from sleeping? Are they ever afraid of things in the night? What do they do when they are afraid? Point out that we can trust Jesus to calm our fears and give us peaceful hearts and minds.

Bulletin Board: "Jesus Gives Peace in a World of Trouble"

1. Cover the board with newspaper.

2. Print the caption and the Bible verse on strips of colored paper and mount them at the top and bottom of the board.

3. Make several copies of the roaring lions pattern on page 24 for children to color and cut out and one copy of Daniel praying.

4. Ask students to name some of the troubles in the world. Print one trouble on each of the lion patterns.

5. Mount Daniel praying at the center of the board and scatter the lions all around him.

6. Pray together for God's peace to replace students' fears.

Jesus Gives Peace in a World of Trouble

SICKNESS SIN CRIME DANGER DEATH WAR

Jesus said, "In me you may have peace. In this world you will have trouble. But take heart! I have overcome the world." (John 16:33)

Peace Crossword

Directions: Fill in the crossword puzzle with the words that complete the Bible verses about God's peace. **A** words go across; **D** words go down.

Therefore, since we have been justified through **1-D**, we have peace with **8-A** through our Lord Jesus Christ. (Romans 5:1)

You will keep in perfect peace him whose **2-A** is steadfast, because he **3-D** in you. (Isaiah 26:3)

Therefore love **3-A** and **4-D**. (Zechariah 8:19b)

A heart at peace gives **5-A** to the body. (Proverbs 14:30)

Great peace have they who **5-D** your law. (Psalm 119:165a)

The Lord **6-A** his people with peace. (Psalm 29:11)

But the meek will inherit the land and **7-D** great peace. (Psalm 37:11)

A Promise of Peace

Directions: Follow the directions below.

1. Read the Bible verse in the first box.

2. Write on the top line who said these words.

3. Draw one line under what He promised to give us.

4. Draw two lines under what He said we should not do.

5. In the second box, write what else He said about peace in John 16:33.

_____ said,

"Peace I leave with you; my peace I give you.

I do not give to you as the world gives. Do not

let your hearts be troubled and do not be afraid."

(John 14:27)

_____

_____

_____

_____

(John 16:33)

What Did He Do?

Directions: Cut out the puzzle pieces. Fit them together to discover what Jesus did to give us peace.

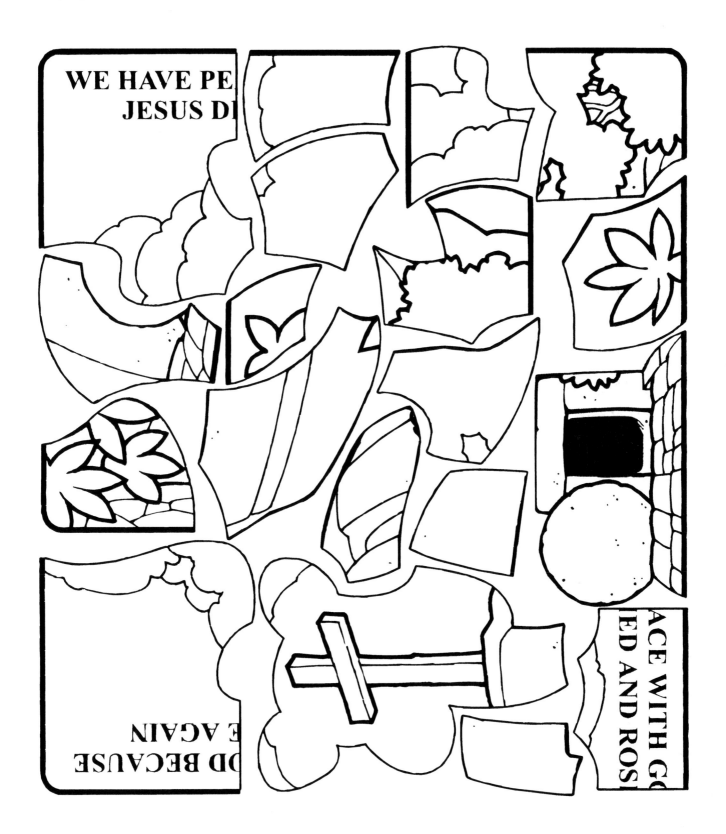

Prince of Peace

Materials

- a copy of the picture on page 29
- black construction paper
- crayons, colored markers, or paints and paintbrushes
- cotton or flannel fabric
- scissors
- glitter
- yarn
- glue sticks

Directions

Have students follow the directions below.

1. Copy and cut out the rectangular picture of Jesus on page 29.
2. Smear glue around the edges of the picture and attach it to a sheet of black construction paper which is slightly larger than the picture for a frame.
3. Color or paint the picture carefully.
4. Cut pieces of fabric the same shape as the clothing.
5. Glue the fabric on Jesus' clothing in the picture.
6. Color or paint the letters of Jesus' name.
7. Smear glue around the figure of Jesus and add glitter.
8. Hold the picture over a waste basket and gently shake off excess glitter.
9. Glue a loop of yarn to the top of the picture for a hanger.
10. Memorize the following rhyme to say when you show the picture to your family and friends.

Jesus is the Prince of Peace

Who died for me and you

And took the punishment for us;

That's what He came to do,

To offer us peace with God

And freedom from our sin.

I have His peace, and you can too

If you'll just ask Him in.

JESUS
THE PRINCE OF PEACE

Let the peace of Christ rule in your hearts.
(Colossians 3:15a)

Bible Story (Job)

Directions: Sing the following story song about Job (based on Job 1–2; 42) for your students; then give them copies and have them sing it with you.

(Tune: "When Johnny Comes Marching Home Again")

In the land of Uz there lived a wealthy man.

His name was Job and all he did was in God's plan.

With seven sons, three daughters, and great flocks and herds and land,

In all the East Job was the very greatest man.

"Have you seen my servant, Job?" God said one day.

"He is blameless and upright and walks My way."

Satan said, "Of course he is; everything he wants is his!

But he'd change his tune if you took it all away."

God knew Job would always love Him and be true,

So to prove to Satan just what Job would do,

Satan took away all he owned and left him with his wife alone.

And Job patiently said, "God, I still praise You"

Satan took away Job's health and gave him pain.

Still he would not disobey; his faith was plain.

His friends said God was punishing him because, of course, Job had sinned,

But Job said, "I'll serve God even if I'm slain!"

Finally, God gave Job another family

And animals and riches so abundantly.

With twice as much as He had before, God blessed Job a whole lot more,

For his faith and patience in *adversity!

(*Note: Explain that the word "adversity" means trouble or difficulty.)

Verse/Bulletin Board

Verse

"You, too, be patient and stand firm, because the Lord's coming is near." (James 5:8)

This verse encourages Christians to be patient as we wait for Jesus to come again. What are some other things about which we need to be patient? Let students share their ideas. Then ask them what James meant when he said that we need to "stand firm." (Stand firm in the faith; live for Jesus and be strong in your Christian testimony.)

Have students say the verse using the following actions:

You, too,	(Move finger, pointing at everyone, even yourself.)
be patient	(Put hands at waist with elbows stuck out.)
and stand firm,	(Stomp feet twice.)
because the Lord's coming	(Point index fingers up as you raise your hands over your head.)
is near.	(Splay hands out and slowly lower arms to your sides.)

Bulletin Board: "Prayer for Patience"

1. Cover the board with light blue paper.

2. Print the caption, prayer poem, and Bible verse on the board as shown.

3. Hand out paper, crayons or markers, and scissors. Have students trace their hands with the fingers together to look like praying hands; then cut them out and sign their names to the hands.

4. Attach the praying hands to the board around the prayer.

5. Ask students to share some situations in which they find it hard to show patience even though they know they need to. (Examples: with younger siblings who are always tagging along; with slower, less capable teammates in sports or games; with older people such as grandparents who don't move quickly; etc.)

6. Pray together, saying the prayer on the board. Then encourage each student to silently ask the Lord to give him or her patience in a specific situation.

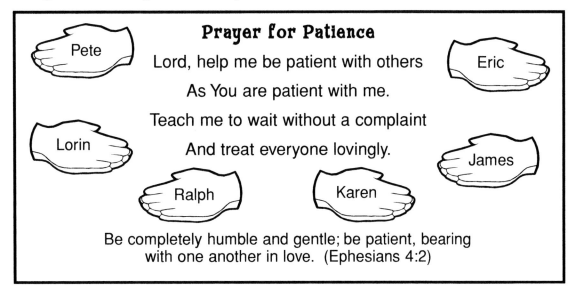

Prayer for Patience

Lord, help me be patient with others

As You are patient with me.

Teach me to wait without a complaint

And treat everyone lovingly.

Be completely humble and gentle; be patient, bearing
with one another in love. (Ephesians 4:2)

Pete   Eric   Lorin   Ralph   Karen   James

A Case of Impatience

Jacob was an Old Testament man who was very impatient. When he and his twin brother Esau were born, God told their mother that the older of the twins (Esau) would serve the younger twin (Jacob). But when Jacob grew up, he just couldn't wait for the Lord to do what He had promised. So, Jacob tricked Esau into giving him the birthright always given to the oldest son.

Directions: Read the story in Genesis 25:29–34. Then write in the story strip below what Jacob and Esau said.

Patient Turtle Craft

Materials

- 2 small paper plates (saucer size)
- the patterns and rhyme on this page
- scissors
- crayons, markers, or paints and paintbrushes
- glue

Directions

1. Color the back of each paper plate green or brown and draw lines on them to make them look like the top and bottom of a turtle shell. (The turtle's top shell should be darker; the bottom one lighter.

2. Color and cut out the turtle head, feet, and tail on this page.

3. Glue the tabs of the head, feet, and tail to the uncolored side of one of the paper plates.

4. Glue the two plates together around the edges with the colored sides out.

5. Cut out the rhyme and glue it to the turtle's back.

6. Read the rhyme. Talk about some times when you get finished quickly and need to wait patiently for others.

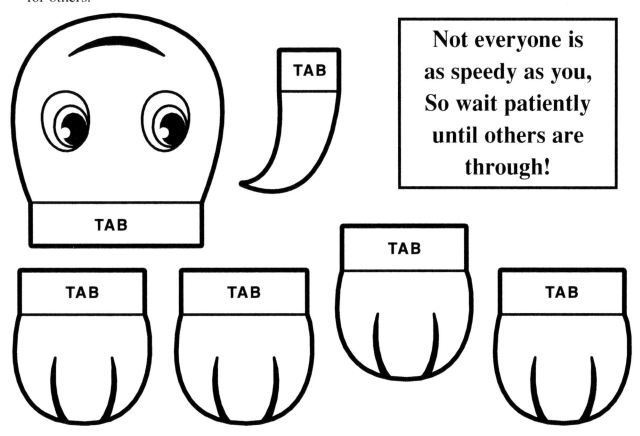

Not everyone is as speedy as you, So wait patiently until others are through!

Patience Puppets

Materials

- puppets on this page
- crayons or markers
- scissors
- transparent tape

Directions

Let students color, cut out, and tape together finger puppets from this page to represent people in their lives—family, friends, neighbors, teachers, classmates, teammates, etc. When the puppets are done, let each student choose a partner. Encourage the partners to work together to use the finger puppets to act out situations where they need to show patience, demonstrating how they would react patiently. After the partners have worked together for awhile, have volunteers perform their finger puppet situations for the whole group. (*Note:* Younger children with smaller hands may need to put two fingers in each puppet.)

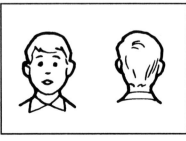  

Patience Rhyme

Directions: Have students act out this rhyme as they say it together, or let them say it while using their finger puppets from page 34.

When you're in a hurry, got someplace to go,
Slow down, take it easy! Have patience—go slow!

When you're waiting on someone who's taking too long,
Instead of getting all uptight, have patience—hum a song!

When a little sister or brother's always there,
Don't tell them to get lost! Have patience, show you care!

Patience isn't easy; but here's a little clue:
Remember all the patience God has shown with you!

Discussion

Talk about how God is patient with you. Do you always obey His Word? Do you pray every day? Do you study the Bible every day? Are you always well-behaved and pay close attention in Sunday School and church?

How Patient?

God had Noah build an ark, a huge boat, in which he and his family and two of every animal would be saved when the earth was flooded. Noah and his family and the animals went into the ark and did not come out again for more than a year! Was Noah a patient man?

Directions

1. Draw a needle on the Patience Gauge to show how patient you think Noah was. (The number 1 is the lowest; the number 10 is the highest.)

2. Write Noah's name on the needle.

3. Read 2 Peter 3:8–9. Peter said that God could have Jesus return anytime, but He is waiting so more people can receive Him as their Savior before it is too late. Is God patient?

4. Draw another needle on the Patience Gauge to show how patient you think God is.

5. Write his name on the needle.

6. How about you? Are you always as patient as you think God would like you to be? Draw a third needle on the Patience Gauge to show how patient you think you are.

7. Write your name on it. Do you need to ask God to help you be more patient?

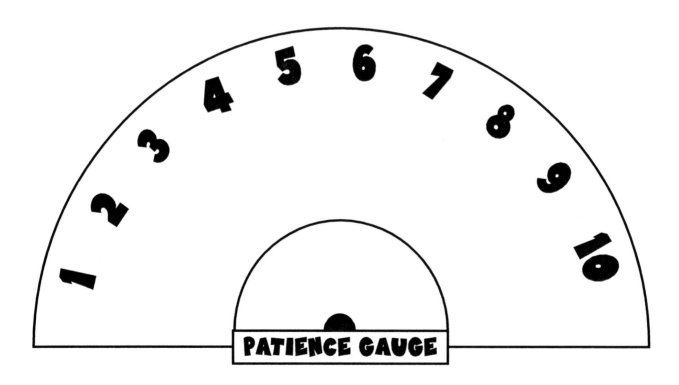

PATIENCE GAUGE

Power of Patience

Directions: Patience is a powerful character trait. To find out what it can do, begin at the arrow and print every other letter in order on the lines below. Look up Proverbs 15:18 (NIV) to check your work.

→ A	0	H	N	0	B	T	U	T	T	E	A	M
P	P	A	E	T	R	I	E	E	D	N	M	T	A
M	N	A	S	N	T	C	I	A	R	L	S	M	U
S	P	A	D	Q	I	U	S	A	S	R	E	R	N
E	S	L	I	X	O	V	N	U	B	D	U	K	T
Z	A	I	P	B	A	G	T	J	I	Y	E	P	N
H	T	F	M	O	A	R	N	D	C	H	A	B	L
P	M	D	S	K	A	B	Q	J	U	O	A	W	R
V	R	G	E	F	L

__ __ __ __ __-__ __ __ __ __ __ __ __

__ __ __ __ __ __ __ __ __

__ __ __ __ __ __ __ __ __ __ , __ __ __ __

__ __ __ __ __ __ __ __ __

__ __ __ __ __ __ __ __ __ __ __ __ .

Why do you think this works?

Bible Story (Rahab)

Directions: Have students pantomime this familiar story of Rahab and the Spies (based on Joshua 2) as you tell it. You will need the following characters: Joshua, two spies, Rahab, King of Jericho, soldiers (the rest of the class). If you have a small class, you can have only two or three soldiers. Set aside a part of your room where the action can take place. Use long strips of paper for the stalks of flax and some rope or a strip of braided cloth for the rope. Two or three chairs next to each other can represent the wall the spies climbed down to get away. Encourage the actors to use a lot of facial expression, as well as physical movement.

Joshua and the Israelites were almost ready to go into the Promised Land, but before he led his people into the land, he decided to send a couple of spies over to check things out. He chose two brave men and said to them, "Go, look over the land, especially Jericho." And so the two spies set off. They walked into the land, making sure they didn't meet anyone who might see they were strangers. They sneaked into the town of Jericho and went to the home of a woman named Rahab. She invited them in, fed them, and made them welcome.

Someone must have seen the two spies and told the King of Jericho. He sent soldiers to Rahab's house with a message. When they came to her door, Rahab quickly took the spies up to the roof and hid them under some stalks of flax. Then she went down, opened the door and received this message from the king: "Bring out the men who came to you and entered your house, because they have come to spy out the whole land."

"There were some men here," Rahab told the soldiers, "but I didn't know where they had come from or why they were here. They left just before the city gate was closed for the night. I don't know which way they went, but you can probably catch them if you hurry!" The soldiers believed Rahab, and they rushed off to try and catch the spies.

When the soldiers had left, Rahab went up to the roof to talk to the two Israelite spies. "I know that God has given you this land," she said to them. "Everyone here is afraid of your people because we heard how the Lord parted the Red Sea and made a dry path for you to walk across it when you escaped out of Egypt. We know that you destroyed the Amorites. The Lord your God is God in heaven above and on the earth below! Please promise me that you will show kindness to me and my family because I have been kind to you. Give me a sign that you will allow us to stay alive when you conquer Jericho."

The two spies told Rahab, "If you don't tell anyone what we are doing, we will treat you kindly and faithfully when the Lord gives us this land. Because you have been kind to us, we will treat you kindly."

Rahab helped the two spies go out a window of her house and climb down a rope to escape over the city wall. "Hide in the hills," she told them, "where the king's soldiers will not find you. Hide for three days and then go on your way."

"When the Israelites enter the land," the men told Rahab, "hang a red cord out your window so we can see it. Bring your family into your house and don't go outside. No matter what happens to the city, everyone in your house will be spared."

"I will do exactly as you say," Rahab told them. And the two spies left without anyone seeing them. They hid in the hills for three days while the king's soldiers looked for them but couldn't find them. Then they went back to the Israelite camp on the other side of the river. They reported to Joshua all that had happened to them. "The Lord has surely given the whole land into our hands," said the spies. "The people are melting in fear because of us!"

Now Joshua knew that it was time to enter the land the Lord had promised Israel.

Verse/Bulletin Board

Verse

"Make sure that nobody pays back wrong for wrong, but always try to be kind to each other and to everyone else." (1 Thessalonians 5:15)

Print on sheets of colored construction paper the words: KINDNESS COUNTS. Put one letter on each sheet of paper. Then turn the paper over and print words and phrases of the memory verse in order on the backs of the letters (K–Make sure; I–that; N–nobody, etc.).

Talk about the importance of kindness. Ask students to imagine what the world would be like without it. Would they want to live in a world without kindness? Hand out the memory verse cards. Challenge students to stand in a line, arranging themselves in order to spell out KINDNESS COUNTS. Then have them turn over the cards to reveal the words of the memory verse. Do this several times, letting students trade letter cards to make it a challenge. To whom does this verse say we should be kind?

Bulletin Board: "Every Day Is Be Kind to Others Day!"

1. Cover the board with white paper.

2. Use red marker to print the caption and the Bible verse on the board as shown.

3. Have students brainstorm ways they can show kindness to friends, schoolmates, their families, neighbors, and the needy. Hand out paper and crayons or markers and have each student draw a picture of himself or herself being kind to someone.

4. When the drawings are done, group them in categories and mount them on the board with category labels.

5. Discuss the situations pictured on the board. Ask students to consider what they will do if they show kindness to someone, but rather than being grateful, the recepient of that kindness responds unkindly. Will students be kind to those who are unkind to them? Have someone read aloud Luke 6:35; then discuss it.

Every Day Is Be Kind to Others Day!

FRIENDS   **SCHOOLMATES**   **THE NEEDY**

FAMILY   **NEIGHBORS**

"Always try to be kind to each other and to everyone else."

(1 Thessalonians 5:15b)

Kind to Whom?

Directions: Read the clues to discover to whom you should be kind. Write the ones the riddles describe in the KINDNESS acrostic below.

Clues

1. Be kind to those who are smaller than you, wherever you are, whatever you do.

2. Be kind to the ones who treat you bad. You may be the only friend they've ever had!

3. They cannot ask for help from you, but they could use a little kindness, too.

4. The person who takes you to school each day deserves your kindness along the way.

5. Always be kind; never be mean to the one who keeps your school so clean.

6. They teach you so much. You really should be kind to them by being good.

7. He preaches and teaches God's Word to you. Show kindness to him and pray for him, too.

8. When they take your money and give your change back, give them a kind word as they hand you your sack.

1. _L_ ___ ___ ___ ___ ___ **K** ___ ___ ___

2. _E_ ___ ___ ___ **I** ___ ___

3. _A_ **N** ___ ___ ___ ___ ___

4. _B_ ___ ___ **D** ___ ___ ___ ___

5. _C_ ___ ___ ___ ___ ___ ___ ___ **N**

6. _T_ **E** ___ ___ ___ ___ ___ ___

7. _P_ ___ **S** ___ ___ ___

8. **S** ___ ___ ___ ___

_C_ ___ ___ ___ ___

Words of Kindness

Directions: One way to show kindness is to say kind, encouraging words to others. The Bible tells us: "An anxious heart weighs a man down, but a kind word cheers him up." (Proverbs 12:25) Draw a line from each situation to the kind words you could say to encourage that person.

1. Your dad catches a big fish.

You can do it!

2. A classmate gets the highest grade on a test.

You did great!

3. A neighbor is sick in the hospital.

You're the best!

4. Your friend's parents get a divorce.

I love you.

5. Your brother or sister is running in a race.

Way to go!

6. Your mom comes home tired after a hard day of work.

You look good!

7. Your teacher is moving away.

I'm praying for you.

8. Your dad is nervous about a job interview.

God loves you and so do I.

9. Your aunt has to have surgery.

Good job!

10. One of your classmates forgets his part in the class play.

Kindness Commandments

Directions: Use the number/letter code to decode the words and complete the sentences.

A	B	C	D	E	F	G	H	I	J	K	L	M
1	2	3	4	5	6	7	8	9	10	11	12	13
N	O	P	Q	R	S	T	U	V	W	X	Y	Z
14	15	16	17	18	19	20	21	22	23	24	25	26

1. Never call people ____ ____ ____ ____ ____.
 14 1 13 5 19

2. Never make ____ ____ ____ of anyone.
 6 21 14

3. Do not ignore anyone, but ____ ____ ____ ____ ____ ____.
 12 9 19 20 5 14

4. Do not be ____ ____ ____ ____, but treat everyone with good manners.
 18 21 4 5

5. Speak only kind, encouraging ____ ____ ____ ____ ____.
 23 15 18 4 19

6. Be ____ ____ ____ ____ ____ ____ ____.
 8 5 12 16 6 21 12

7. ____ ____ ____ ____ ____ ____ people as they are.
 1 3 3 5 16 20

8. Do not criticize or put people ____ ____ ____ ____.
 4 15 23 14

9. Be kind, even to people who are ____ ____ ____ ____ ____ ____ to you.
 21 14 11 9 14 4

10. Treat other people the way ____ ____ ____ would like to be treated.
 25 15 21

Directions: Give each student an 8 ½" x 11" (22 cm x 28 cm) sheet of paper, crayons, scissors, and glue. Have them color the whole sheet with several different bright colors. Have students color the pattern below black, leaving the designs white. Then have them cut out the window and carefully cut out the designs on the window. They will need sharp, pointed scissors for this task. (You or a helper will need to do this for younger students.) Show them how to glue the window on the colored paper so the colors show through the designs. Then have them trim the colored paper the same size as the window.

Kindness Cards

Directions: Talk about how giving cards to people is a way to show kindness. These may be cards that say "Thank-you," "Have a good day," "Get well soon," "I'm praying for you," "I love you," or just "Hello." Let students color and cut out the two-sided card below and fold it in half along the broken line. They can glue a piece of string on for the tail. Have them decide who they want to give the card to, then print their message on it. (Examples: Outside—A Great Big Thank You! Inside—Thanks for your kindness.; Outside—Have a great big, Inside—wonderful day!) Encourage students to include something about God's love in their personal messages.

Kindness Chain

Discuss with students how kindness often has a chain reaction. When you are kind to someone, that person is more likely to go and be kind to someone else; then that person shows kindness to someone, and so on until many people benefit from your kindness. Why are we more likely to be kind to other people when kindness has been shown to us? Being treated kindly makes us feel good and feeling good makes us want to share that good feeling with those around us. How does God show kindness to us? Does His kindness make you want to show kindness to others? That's the way He wants it. Read Ephesians 4:32. God set the example of kindness for us. Now he wants us to spread His kindness around.

There is a true story about a man who was driving along the highway one night when he saw a car pulled over to the side of the road with a flat tire. He pulled out of the lanes of traffic rushing by and stopped behind the car. A woman with her young child were inside. "I would call my husband, but I forgot my cell phone," she told him. The man kindly took off the flat tire and put on the spare. When the woman tried to give him some money the man said, "No, I don't want any money. If you'll just show kindness to someone else in the days ahead, that will be payment enough for me." Then he got back in his car and drove away. A few weeks later the man was driving down the highway in a heavy rainstorm when his tires hit a slick patch and his car swerved off the road and into a ditch. He tried to drive the car back onto the road, but the tires were stuck in the mud. Suddenly, he saw a tow truck pull over. The driver got out and said to him, "You look like you could use some help." Then he hooked onto the man's car and quickly pulled it out of the ditch. When the man tried to give the tow truck driver some money, he was told, "Thanks, but I don't want money. My wife had a flat tire near here a few weeks ago. She and my little boy were scared and didn't know what to do because they didn't have the cell phone with them. Then a very kind man stopped and changed the tire for her. He wouldn't take any money. He told her to just show kindness to someone else, so that's what I'm doing."

Give students strips of colored construction paper about 8 ½" x ¾" (22 cm x 2 cm). Have students write on the strips kindnesses others have shown them as well as kind deeds they have done. Show them how to tape or glue the ends of the strips together to form chain links. Link them all together into a long chain. Hang the kindness chain on the wall. Continue to add paper links to the chain as students report kind deeds done for them and they do kind deeds for others.

Teach students this song to help them remember the importance of showing kindness.

(Tune: "B-I-N-G-O")

Be kind to everyone you meet

As God is kind to you.

Be K-I-N-D,

Be K-I-N-D,

Be K-I-N-D,

As God is kind to you.

Bible Story (Josiah)

Directions: Read the action rhyme about King Josiah (based on 2 Kings 22–23) and do the actions. Have students copy your actions and repeat the recurring line.

Josiah was a little boy; he was only eight
(Hold up hand to indicate short stature.)
When he became Judah's king, but God made him great!
(Point up to heaven; then hold up both fists.)
He was good and always would
Do what was right in God's sight.
When the Book of God, which had been lost for many years,
(Open hands like an open book.)
Was found and read to him, Josiah was in tears.
(Put face in hands as if crying.)
He was good and always would
Do what was right in God's sight.
Josiah learned that he and everyone had disobeyed.
(Bow down as if in prayer.)
What would happen to them all? Josiah was afraid!
(Shake as if afraid.)
He was good and always would
Do what was right in God's sight.
King Josiah had God's Law read to everyone.
(Open hands like an open book; hold them up high.)
They all pledged to obey it, but the king had just begun!
(Hold right hand over heart.)
He was good and always would
Do what was right in God's sight.
Josiah tore down idols and shrines and sacred stones.
(Smack fists together.)
He wanted everyone to worship God and God alone!
(Raise hands toward heaven.)
He was good and always would
Do what was right in God's sight.
They celebrated Passover, forgotten for so long,
(Hold hands with others.)
Josiah did all he could do to right the country's wrongs.
(Make thumbs-up gesture with both hands.)
He was good and always would
Do what was right in God's sight.
The Bible says Josiah was like no other king.
(Hold out arms as if welcoming or accepting others.)
He turned to the Lord and followed Him in everything!
(Bow head.)
He was good and always would
Do what was right in God's sight.

Verse/Bulletin Board

Verse

"Love must be sincere. Hate what is evil; cling to what is good." (Romans 12:9)

Point out that goodness has two parts to it: hating evil and clinging to good. The dictionary defines goodness as: purity, honesty, honor, innocence, kindness, generosity. Goodness is all that and more because goodness is being like Josiah, living for the Lord with all your heart and soul and strength. Trying to be good on our own doesn't last; our goodness must come from God who originated it!

Cut a heart shape from red paper, a square from black paper, and a circle from yellow paper. Print the three parts of the memory verse on the three shapes:

red heart	Love must be sincere.
black square	Hate what is evil;
yellow circle	cling to what is good.

Hold up the three shapes and have students read the words on them. Then turn one of the shapes over to the blank side. Let students try to say the verse, filling in the missing words. Turn that shape back to the word side; turn another shape over to the blank side and have students say the verse again. After a while, hold up all the blank sides of the shapes and see if students can say the verse. Then let them try saying it without any of the shapes to prompt them.

Bulletin Board: "Be a Shining Example of Goodness!"

1. Cover the board with white paper.

2. Use black marker to print the caption and the Bible verse on the board as shown.

3. On the right side of the board, let students use colored markers to print ways to demonstrate goodness in the areas mentioned in the verse: in speech—Jesus loves you! Can I help you?; in life—obey parents, etc.

4. Use yellow crayon or chalk to draw a rising sun at the bottom of the board with rays extending up to the top of the board, going over the words of the verse and children's ideas.

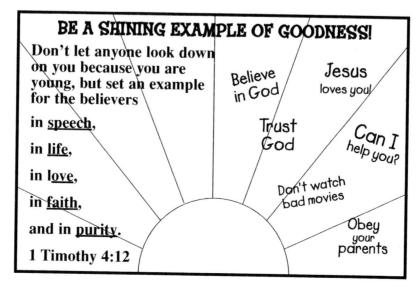

Shine Like Stars

Directions: Paul wrote to Christians in the town of Philippi that he wanted them to become the following:

" . . .blameless and pure, children of God without fault in a crooked and depraved generation, in which you shine like stars in the universe." (Philippians 2:15, NIV)

Find three descriptions of Christians Paul wrote in this verse. Write them on three of the stars. Think of some other words that describe Christians and write them on the other stars.

Pleasing God

Directions: Read the Bible verses in the box. Then follow the directions for marking them.

"For you were once darkness,

but now you are light in the Lord.

Live as children of light

(for the fruit of the light consists in all goodness, righteousness and truth)

and find out what pleases the Lord."

Ephesians 5:8–10

---

1. Draw one line under what you used to be.

2. Draw two lines under what you are now. What do you think caused this change?

_____

_____

3. Circle how you are to live now. What does this mean in your everyday life?

_____

_____

4. How can you do what the last line tells you to do?

_____

_____

Puppet Skit

Directions: Let students make their own sheep puppets using the patterns and directions on page 51. They can use the puppets to act out the skit on this page. You will need to provide paper lunch bags (preferably white), copies of the patterns, scissors, glue, crayons, and cotton balls.

Divide students into good sheep and bad sheep for the skit based on Luke 15:1–6. Assign speaking parts. You should read the part of the Shepherd.

All sheep: Baa! Baa! Baa!

Good Sheep 1: What a beautiful day! I can hardly wait to see where the shepherd leads us today!

All Good Sheep: (happily) Baa! That's right! We can't wait! Baa!

Bad Sheep 1: (angrily) Baa! Who cares where the shepherd wants us to go! We've already decided what we want to do.

All Bad Sheep: (angrily) Baa! You got that right! We'll do what we want! Baa!

Good Sheep 2: But our shepherd knows what's best for us. He always leads us to the greenest grass and the freshest water.

All Good Sheep: Yes! We can trust him! He's never treated us Baa-dly.

Bad Sheep 2: (angrily) Baa! There's a lot of stuff he never lets us do and places he won't let us go. And we're not going to let him run our lives!

All Bad Sheep: (angrily) Baa! We want to do our own thing! Baa! He doesn't care about us!

Good Sheep 3: Of course he does! He keeps us safe and takes care of us. Why, he would give his own life for us!

All Good Sheep: Our shepherd loves all his sheep!

Bad Sheep 3: Well, this little sheep is going to be Baa-d today! (laugh) Anybody want to join me in a little straying?

All Bad Sheep: Uh, maybe tomorrow.

Bad Sheep 3: I don't care. See you later!

Shepherd: Good morning, little flock. Are you ready for this good day? Wait, is someone missing? Yes, one sheep has gone astray. I must go look for him before he runs into trouble. Stay here. I'll be back as soon as I find him.

All Sheep: (Upset) Baa! This is Baa-d!

Bad Sheep 3: Baa! This is a way I've never been before. Just look at that green grass down there! Boy, am I going to have a feast! And it's all mine! Wait! I'm falling! Help! My foot is caught in the rocks. How will I ever get back up the hill? What if a wolf finds me? Baa! Baa!

Shepherd: Little sheep? There you are. I've been searching for you for hours! How did you get down there? Just calm down. I'll come and rescue you.

Bad Sheep 3: (Scared) Baa! Baa! Baa!

Shepherd: Hold still. You'll be fine. I'll just carry you on my shoulders back to the flock.

All Sheep: Baa! Baa! Are you okay? What happened? Are you hurt Baa-dly?

Bad Sheep 3: The shepherd came and rescued me. From now on I'll obey the shepherd because I know he really loves me. I want to follow him and please him because I love him too.

All Sheep: Baa! Baa! Welcome Baa-ck!

Shepherd: Jesus, the Good Shepherd, loves you and wants you to follow Him. He will fill you with His goodness and love. He died for you. Will you live for Him?

Sheep Puppet

Directions

1. Cut out the patterns on this page.

2. Color the sheep's eyes and mouth.

3. Glue the sheep's head on the flat bottom of a paper lunch bag.

4. Glue the mouth pattern on the side of the bag under the flat bottom.

5. Pull cotton balls apart and glue the cotton bits on the sheep's head and the paper bag.

6. Put your hand inside the bag and move it to make it look like the sheep is talking.

Goodness Door Strip

Materials

- copies of this page and page 53
- crayons or colored markers
- clear plastic adhesive
- 36" (91 cm) long strips of wide ribbon or crepe paper
- scissors
- yarn
- glue

Directions

1. Give each student a copy of this page and page 53.
2. Have students color all ten squares, then cut them apart.
3. Show students how to cover each square with clear plastic adhesive to protect it.
4. Have them glue the 10 squares in order down the ribbon or crepe paper strip.
5. Glue a small loop of yarn at the top for a hanger.
6. Read the squares together and discuss them. Have students take them home to hang on their doors as reminders of how to demonstrate goodness in their lives.

WHAT IS GOODNESS?

GENEROSITY
Do good, be rich in good deeds, be generous and willing to share. (See 1 Timothy 6:18.)

OBEDIENCE
Whoever has my commands and obeys them, he is the one who loves me. (John 14:21a)

OFFERING HELP
Be like Dorcas. Do good and help the poor. (See Acts 9:36.)

Goodness Door Strip

DETERMINATION
Stand firm. Let nothing move you. Always give yourselves fully to the work of the Lord. (See 1 Corinthians 15:58.)

NEW BIRTH
We know that anyone born of God does not continue to sin. (1 John 5:18a)

ENDURANCE
We work hard with our own hands. When we are cursed, we bless; when we are persecuted, we endure it. (1 Corinthians 4:12)

SERVICE
Serve one another in love. (See Galatians 5:13.)

SPIRIT'S GIFT
The fruit of the Spirit is love, joy, peace, patience, kindness, goodness, faithfulness (Galatians 5:22)

Lord, fill me with Your

goodness, and make it

overflow

On everybody I'm around,

Everywhere I go.

Bible Story (Esther)

Directions: To tell this story of Queen Esther (based on Esther 2–9), cut out a paper crown and wear it when talking about Queen Esther or the king.

(Put on crown.) The great king of Persia was looking for a new queen. His attendants began looking for beautiful young women. The one who pleased the king the most would be chosen queen. *(Take off crown.)* A godly Jew named Mordecai heard what was happening and decided his young cousin Esther would make a perfect queen. He had raised Esther after her parents had died and no one could deny that she was beautiful. Mordecai convinced Esther to join the group of women at the palace. The attendant in charge liked Esther, and he made sure she received special food and all kinds of beauty treatments.

Everyone who met Esther saw that she was good, as well as beautiful. She was Jewish, but Mordecai warned her not to tell anyone. Mordecai came by every day to find out how Esther was. She was in the palace for a whole year before she got to see the king. When they finally met, he was more attracted to Esther than to any of the other young women. It didn't take him long to decide to make Esther his queen. *(Put on crown.)* He set a royal crown on her head, then gave a great banquet to celebrate the occasion. He even proclaimed a holiday throughout the land and gave gifts to everyone. *(Take off crown.)*

One of the king's officials was a wicked man named Haman. The royal officials bowed down to honor Haman, but Mordecai, standing nearby, would not bow down. Mordecai would bow to no one but God. This made Haman very angry. When he found out that Mordecai was a Jew, Haman planned a way to not only get his revenge on the man, but also destroy all the Jews in the land. He told the king, "There is a group of people in this land whose customs are different from everyone else's. They refuse to obey the laws. They really should be eliminated before they cause problems. If you, oh King, will make a decree to destroy them, I will see that it is carried out."

(Put on crown.) The king foolishly agreed without even looking into the matter. "Do what you please with those people," he told Haman. *(Take off crown.)* Wicked Haman immediately began sending out orders to destroy all the Jews in the land on a certain day.

When Mordecai heard about this, he tore his clothes and cried. All the Jews in the land were mourning and fasting (eating no food) and crying. *(Put on crown.)* When Queen Esther's maidens told her about Mordecai's distress, she

sent a messenger to find out what was wrong. Mordecai explained what Haman had done. He sent Esther a copy of the decree Haman had written. Then he told the queen's messenger to urge her to talk to the king and beg him to spare the lives of her people.

When Esther read the decree and heard Mordecai's words, she was very upset. As queen of the land she had little real power. A law stated that anyone who approached the king without being invited could be put to death—even the queen—unless the king showed by his raised scepter that her life should be spared.

She had not seen the king for a month. It would be extremely dangerous for her to go see him without being invited. Esther sent word to Mordecai, explaining her situation. He sent back this message to her: "Do not think that because you are in the king's house you alone of all the Jews will escape. For if you remain silent at this time, relief and deliverance for the Jews will arise from another place, but you and your father's family will perish. And who knows but that you have come to royal position for such a time as this?" When Esther received his message, she asked her cousin to get all the Jews in town to pray and fast for her for three days. She and her maidens would do the same. Then she would go talk to the king.

Three days later, Esther put on her royal robes and went to see the king. He raised his scepter and welcomed her. Esther invited the king to a special banquet and asked him to bring Haman. Instead of telling the king what she wanted at the banquet, Esther invited him and Haman to another banquet the next day. *(Take off crown.)* By this time, Haman was feeling pretty proud of himself. Then on his way home he saw Mordecai and became angry all over again, but he soothed himself with the knowledge that Mordecai and all the Jews would soon be dead. *(Put on crown.)* The next day at the queen's banquet, she revealed that she was a Jew; then told the king what Haman was doing to her and her people. The king was so angry he had Haman put to death. The king could not change the law to have the Jews destroyed, but he sent out another decree on behalf of the Jews so that they were able to destroy their enemies instead of the other way around. Because of Esther's faithfulness, even when her life was in danger, her people were saved.

Verse/Bulletin Board

Verse

"But be sure to fear the Lord and serve him faithfully with all your heart." (1 Samuel 12:24)

Ask students to share their ideas about what it means to serve the Lord faithfully. Remind them that faithfulness is a gift of the Holy Spirit. We can only serve the Lord faithfully when we allow the Holy Spirit to be in charge. If we try to be faithful on our own without His help, we will fail every time.

Point out that serving the Lord faithfully means always following where He leads. Trace around your feet and make 11 footprint shapes. Print a word or two of the memory verse on each footprint. Print the verse reference on the last footprint. After cutting them out, put rolled up masking tape on the back of each footprint and attach them in a path on the floor on one side of the room. Have students say the words as they step on the footprints.

Bulletin Board: "Faithfulness Is a Daily Thing"

1. Cover the board with light green paper.

2. Print the caption, the rhyming prayer, and the Bible verse on the board as shown.

3. Scatter pages of old calendars all around the board.

4. Have a time of prayer, inviting students to say the rhyming prayer on the board to God.

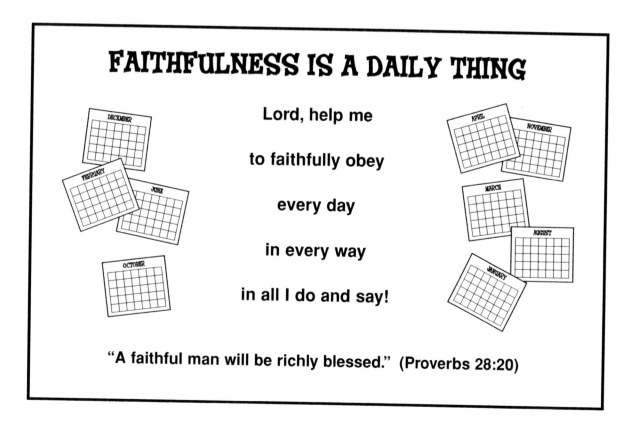

FAITHFULNESS IS A DAILY THING

Lord, help me

to faithfully obey

every day

in every way

in all I do and say!

"A faithful man will be richly blessed." (Proverbs 28:20)

God Is Faithful

Directions: If you want to see how faithfulness works, study the Bible to get a picture of God's faithfulness to us. Look up the verses and fill in the missing words. Then find and circle those words in the puzzle.

1. The Lord is faithful to _____ his _____ and loving toward all he has made. (Psalm 145:13b)

2. Blessed is he whose help is . . . the Maker of heaven and earth, the sea, and everything in them—the Lord, who remains faithful _____. (Psalm 146:5–6)

3. I will _____ leave you nor forsake you. (Joshua 1:5b)

4. His faithfulness continues through all _____. (Psalm 100:5b)

5. For I am convinced that neither _____ nor life, neither angels nor demons, neither the present nor the _____, nor any _____, neither height nor depth, nor _____ else in all creation, will be able to separate us from the love of God that is in Christ Jesus our Lord. (Romans 8:38–39)

L	I	K	N	P	Z	Q	L	R	B
F	U	T	U	R	E	S	N	G	G
S	B	N	F	O	R	E	V	E	R
V	Q	N	R	M	Q	B	Z	N	J
J	L	E	M	I	D	Z	Y	E	P
V	L	V	D	S	Z	Z	J	R	O
Y	W	E	Q	E	X	C	J	A	W
X	B	R	Z	S	A	V	V	T	E
A	Y	B	J	Z	T	T	Z	I	R
W	L	Z	B	Q	J	Z	H	O	S
Q	R	L	R	B	C	P	S	N	D
A	N	Y	T	H	I	N	G	S	G

Faithfulness Song

Directions: Teach students this song. Sing it together with lots of hand clapping and foot stomping.

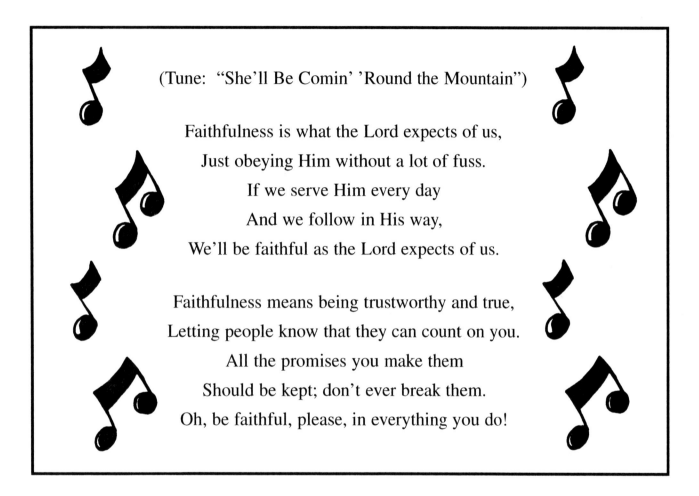

(Tune: "She'll Be Comin' 'Round the Mountain")

Faithfulness is what the Lord expects of us,
Just obeying Him without a lot of fuss.
If we serve Him every day
And we follow in His way,
We'll be faithful as the Lord expects of us.

Faithfulness means being trustworthy and true,
Letting people know that they can count on you.
All the promises you make them
Should be kept; don't ever break them.
Oh, be faithful, please, in everything you do!

Activity

1. Sing the first stanza of the song, then while you are all still clapping your hands to the rhythm, ask students to suggest specific ways they can serve God and follow in His way (such as going to church, reading the Bible, praying, etc.).

2. After a student suggests something, have everyone repeat it to the rhythm of the song.

3. Sing the second stanza, then continue clapping while you have students suggest specific ways they can show people they can count on them (such as being a loyal friend, helping, etc.)

4. Again, after a student suggests something, have everyone repeat it to the rhythm. Then sing the whole song again.

Faithful People

Directions: See if you can match the faithful people with their descriptions. If you need help, look up the Bible verses.

_____ 1. I faithfully followed my mother-in-law to her land and cared for her.

A. Stephen (Acts 7:54–58)

_____ 2. We were thrown into a fiery furnace for being faithful to God!

B. Ruth (Ruth 1:16–18)

_____ 3. I faithfully obeyed God, and my family and I were saved from drowning.

C. Joshua (Joshua 6)

_____ 4. I was faithful to God in Egypt, and God used me to save my family from starving.

D. Noah (Genesis 6:22)

_____ 5. I faithfully preached in many countries and wrote letters to churches to help them grow in Christ.

E. Shadrach, Meshach, and Abednego (Daniel 3)

_____ 6. I served as one of Jesus' disciples and wrote five books in the Bible, including the last one.

F. John (Revelation 1:1)

_____ 7. I obeyed God's strange instructions and conquered the city of Jericho.

G. Joseph (Genesis 45:7–8)

_____ 8. I faithfully preached God's truth and was stoned to death by an angry mob.

H. Paul (Acts 28:30–31)

Faithfulness Magnet

Materials

- pattern from this page
- colored markers or crayons
- gummed gold and silver stars
- rickrack or decorative cord
- plastic lids from frosting containers (or 3½" [9 cm] diameter lids from other containers)
- scissors
- construction paper
- glue
- magnetic strips

Directions

1. Give each student a 3½" (9 cm) diameter lid.

2. Have them trace the lid on construction paper (a color of their choice), then cut out the circle and glue it to the inside of the lid.

3. Give each student the pattern below to color and cut out.

4. Have them glue the pattern over the construction paper on the inside of the lid.

5. Let them stick gold and silver stars on the pattern.

6. Show them how to glue rickrack or cord around the outside of the lid to decorate it.

7. Cut magnetic strips into smaller pieces. Give one to each student to glue on the back of his or her decorated lid.

8. Read the message on the magnet and talk about it. Read the adjectives around the rim. Ask students if they think those words describe God. Do the words also describe them?

9. Let students take their magnets home to put on their refrigerators to grab the attention of everyone in the family.

Three Faithful Men

King Nebuchadnezzar had a huge gold statue of himself built. Then he called all his officials together and told them that everyone must bow before his statue and worship it when they heard the musical signal. But there were three men who remained faithful to God. Shadrach, Meshach, and Abednego refused to bow down before the statue. This made the king furious! He ordered that they be brought before him. "Is it true that you refuse to worship my statue?" he asked them. He warned them that if they did not bow down to the gold statue, he would have them thrown into a fiery furnace!

"If you throw us into a fiery furnace for not worshiping your statue," the three men told the king, "the God we serve is able to save us. But even if He does not choose to, we will still not bow down and worship anyone or anything but God!" This made King Nebuchadnezzar so angry, he ordered the fiery furnace to be heated seven times hotter. Then he told his strongest soldiers to tie up Shadrach, Meshach, and Abednego and throw them into the furnace. What happened to the three faithful men who were thrown into the furnace?

Directions: Complete the picture to show what the king saw when he looked into the furnace. Read Daniel 3:24–27 if you need help.

60

Following Him

Directions: Faithfully following the Lord is not easy. There are many ways Satan tries to distract us and get us headed in the wrong direction. Find your way through the maze to Jesus' words of encouragement. Don't let anything get you off the right path!

Bible Story (Solomon)

Directions: As you tell this story of King Solomon (based on 1 Kings 3; Proverbs 15:1, 18), ask questions and allow time for students to answer.

Do you know who was the greatest king Israel every had? *(Let students answer.)* King David loved God and served him faithfully. He is known as Israel's greatest king. When David died, his son Solomon became king. For what was Solomon known? *(Let students answer.)* When Solomon became king, the Lord spoke to him in a dream: "Ask for whatever you want me to give you." Solomon could have asked for anything—riches, power, honor, fame! But Solomon told God that he needed wisdom, an understanding heart, to be a good king. He confessed to God, "I am only a little child and do not know how to carry out my duties." He could not be the kind of king Israel needed without God's help.

Have you ever felt helpless, like you couldn't do what you were supposed to do? *(Let students answer.)* Then you know how Solomon felt. Would having a lot of money make him a good king? *(Let students answer.)* Would great power help him make right decisions for the country? *(Let students answer.)* No, what he needed was great wisdom. And that's what God gave him. God was pleased with Solomon's request. In fact, He promised not only to give Solomon the wisdom he asked for, but also the riches and honor and power he didn't ask for, as well as a long life. God said there would never be another king like Solomon.

Solomon was a gentle king. He used his wisdom instead of force. Once two women came to him and asked him to solve their problem. Both women had newborn babies at the same time, but one of the babies had died. One night the woman whose baby had died stole the baby of the other woman while she was sleeping and put the dead baby in her bed! Now they were arguing about who was the real mother of the living baby. They wanted Solomon to decide. How in the world could Solomon know who the real mother was? What could he do? *(Let students answer.)* He used his wisdom to think of a gentle way to solve the problem. He had a sword brought and gave the order for the living baby to be cut in half so the women could share him.

Do you think Solomon really intended to kill the baby? *(Let students answer.)* No, of course not. But the two women didn't know that. One of the women said, "No, please, don't kill him! Let her have him, but let him live." The other woman said, "That's a good idea. Cut the baby in half, then neither of us shall have him." Which woman do you think was the baby's real mother? *(Let students answer.)* Solomon immediately knew that the baby's real mother was the woman who loved him so much she was willing to give him up rather than see him killed. So Solomon ordered that the baby should be given to her.

Do you know what Bible books Solomon wrote? *(Let students answer.)* One of the books he wrote was Proverbs. *(Have students turn to Proverbs in their Bibles.)* A proverb is a wise saying and since Solomon was so wise, he had lots of good advice and lessons to teach us. One of the things he wrote about was gentleness. Turn to Proverbs 15:1. Let's read it together. Do you think that statement is true? Solomon knew what he was talking about, didn't he? He must have known this by experience. Perhaps when his officials became angry and argued with one another, he spoke a gentle word to them to calm them down and cool them off. Have you ever stopped someone from being angry by speaking gentle words to them? *(Let students answer.)* Why do you think gentleness works this way? *(Let students answer.)* Look at Proverbs 15:18. Let's read it together. The word used here is *patient*, but we can see that again Solomon is talking about the way a gentle person deals with others, not arguing or fighting but trying to bring peace.

What do Solomon's proverbs tell us about the kind of person he was? *(Let students answer.)* He is famous for being a wise and gentle king who built a great temple for the Lord, not for the military battles he led or the enemies he defeated. Those were his greatest accomplishments.

Verse

"Be completely humble and gentle; be patient, bearing with one another in love." (Ephesians 4:2)

Discuss what it means to be gentle. People sometimes think gentleness is weakness, but gentleness is really a wonderful strength. Jesus was gentle, but never weak. Ask students how much gentleness God wants us to display in our lives. Point out that the verse says to be "completely" humble and gentle. That means all the time, not just now and then. One of the ways the dictionary defines *gentle* is "free from harshness, sternness, or violence." Gentleness is a softness of attitude that brings calm and peace to those around you. Ask students to name some gentle people they know.

Print the following word search puzzle on the chalkboard. Let students take turns finding and circling the 13 words from the Bible verse in order in the puzzle.

C	E	B	E	J	H	S	W
O	N	H	U	M	B	L	E
M	A	O	Z	G	E	E	P
P	Z	N	R	E	A	Q	A
L	L	E	D	N	R	B	T
E	O	J	B	T	I	Z	I
T	V	V	Z	L	N	Q	E
E	Q	R	E	E	G	I	N
L	Z	L	W	I	T	H	T
Y	A	N	O	T	H	E	R

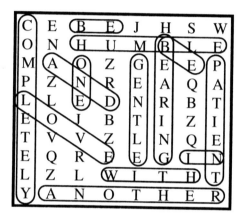

Bulletin Board: "A Gentle Answer Turns Away Anger"

1. Cover the board with light blue paper.

2. Print the Bible verse at the top of the board.

3. Enlarge the dog and cat patterns on page 64.

4. Color them and cut them out.

5. Mount the dog and cat at the center of the board.

6. Hand out paper and crayons or markers.

7. Have students draw pictures of themselves calming angry people with a gentle response.

8. Scatter them around the board.

A GENTLE ANSWER TURNS AWAY ANGER

Bulletin Board Patterns

Be Gentle

Directions: Decode the Bible verse. Then look up Philippians 4:5 in your Bible to check your work. What do you think this verse means?

CODE

A	B	C	D	E	F	G	H	I	J	K	L	M
○	▯	▱	⋈	△	☾	✚	⟷	☆	+	◐	⌒	☽

N	O	P	Q	R	S	T	U	V	W	X	Y	Z
⌣	⇧	∫∫	⊖	▯	▢	△	◣	⌂	◎	▮	◉	⇩

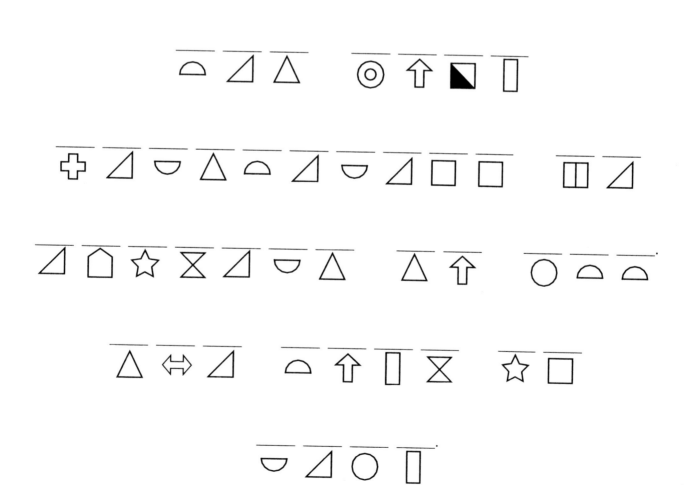

Gentle Jesus

Directions: Jesus described Himself as gentle. Read His words in Matthew 11:28–30. Then fill in the missing words in the verses below and in the acrostic.

Come to me, all you who are _____ and
6

_____ , and I will _____
3   1

you _____ . _____ my yoke upon
9   4

you and _____ from me, for I am gentle and
7

_____ in _____ , and you will
5   2

find rest for your _____ . For my yoke is
10

_____ and my burden is light.
8

1. **G** ____ ____ ____

2. ____ **E** ____ ____ ____

3. ____ ____ ____ ____ ____ **N** ____ ____

4. **T** ____ ____ ____

5. ____ ____ ____ ____ **L** ____

6. ____ **E** ____ ____ ____

7. ____ ____ ____ ____ **N**

8. **E** ____ ____ ____

9. ____ ____ **S** ____

10. **S** ____ ____ ____ ____

Gentle Living

"I walk lightly and bend you over, so when I leave you can stand up again."
(A Native American saying)

This Native American quote shows the desire to walk gently on the earth, not harming anything, even being careful where and how they walk rather than tromp down the grass. Many of the creatures God created are smaller and weaker than we are. How we treat them sometimes shows how we also treat people. Here are some things to think about.

- When you find a caterpillar, do you step on it? What should you do instead?

- How do you treat the pets in your house that depend on you?

- How do you treat students at school who have a hard time learning? Do you make friends with those who are different?

Directions

1. Write on three of the footsteps some ways you can respect the earth by "walking" or living with gentleness.

2. Write on the other three footsteps some ways you can encourage other people by treating them gently. (Think of people with whom you do not usually spend a lot of time.)

3. Read Romans 13:10. God would like all of us to be "harmless," not hurting others but helping.

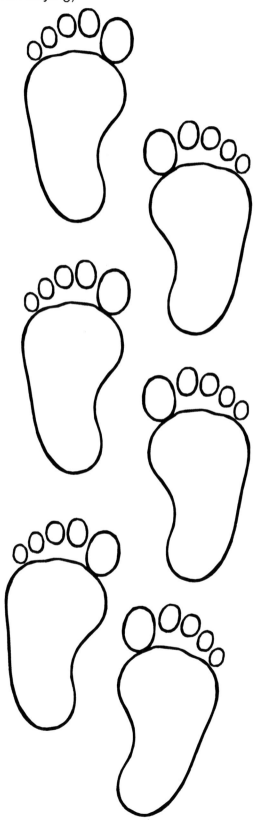

Gentle as a Lamb

Materials

- copies of the lamb pattern on page 69
- poster board or lightweight cardboard
- white paint and small paintbrushes
- scissors
- black markers
- newspapers
- cotton balls
- glue
- transparent tape

Directions

1. Have students trace the lamb pattern on poster board or lightweight cardboard and cut it out.

2. Cover a table with newspapers to protect the table. Have students paint their lambs with white paint.

3. Have them use black markers to draw the eyes, nose, ears, and other features on both sides of the lamb.

4. Have them fold the lamb on the broken line to make it stand up. If the lamb doesn't stand, have students tape a strip of cardboard at the bottom to hold the two sides together and keep them from slipping. Then have them glue bits of cotton balls on both sides of the lamb.

5. Teach them the song below. Let them move their lambs around (running, leaping, etc.) as they sing the song. The lambs will be a reminder of Jesus' gentleness and the gentleness He wants us to show to others.

(Tune: "Mary Had a Little Lamb")

Jesus is the Lamb of God,

Lamb of God, Lamb of God.

Jesus is the Lamb of God

Who died for you and me.

Jesus gently shared God's love,

Shared God's love, shared God's love.

Jesus gently shared God's love;

A gentle lamb was He.

When we give our lives to Him,

Lives to Him, lives to Him,

When we give our lives to Him,

How gentle we can be!

Jesus, make us gentle lambs,

Gentle lambs, gentle lambs.

Jesus, make us gentle lambs

To serve you faithfully.

Lamb Pattern

#7029 Fruit of the Spirit

Bible Story (David)

Directions: Set up the following stations around the room:

1. a table for students to sit around with a snack to eat (such as fruit or crackers) as you talk
2. an area at the back of the room to represent the field where Jonathan and David met (If possible, have a small bow with rubber tipped arrows to shoot at this station.)
3. a table or some chairs covered with a blanket to represent the cave where David cut Saul's robe
4. an empty area in which students may lie down to represent Hakilah

Walk around the room as you tell the story of David running from Saul (based on 1 Samuel 19–24; 26), taking the children with you to these stations to make the story come alive.

Saul was the king of all Israel, but he was jealous of David. Everyone talked about David, people sang of his success in battles, women admired him, children shouted when he walked by, and everyone loved him. Saul was so jealous he decided to kill him and David heard about it. Saul's son Jonathan and David made a plan to find out if Saul was really out to get him. David would not come to eat with them at the New Moon Festival. Jonathan would meet him later and let him know what Saul said about him. They arranged to meet in a field where Jonathan would be practicing his archery. *(Take students to station 1 and pass out a snack.)* So Jonathan sat down to the meal with his father without his friend David. Saul said nothing, so Jonathan thought his intention to kill David must not be true. But the next day when David was not at the meal again, Saul asked his son about him as they ate. Jonathan made an excuse for him. Suddenly, Saul began yelling at his son in anger, "Don't you know that as long as David is alive, you will never get to be king? Bring David to me so I can kill him!"

"Why should David have to die? He's done nothing!" Jonathan said. Saul was so mad he threw a spear at his own son. Jonathan left the table. He couldn't eat, he was so sad to see how his father felt about his best friend. The next morning Jonathan went to the field with his bow and arrow to meet David. *(Take students to station 2 and shoot some arrows.)* He began shooting arrows and told the boy with him to run and find his arrows after he shot them. He shouted directions to the boy which were a pre-arranged signal to tell David to run away because Saul wanted to kill him. After saying goodbye to his best friend, David left to try to escape Saul.

For years, David ran from Saul. Some of David's friends and family came to stay with him in caves and in forests, traveling over hills and mountains, constantly in danger. Just when David would start to relax, the king and his army would appear and David would have to run again. He could have killed Saul at any time, but he wouldn't do it. David knew he was going to be king someday. He trusted God to work things out. *(Take students to station 3. Let some of them crawl into the "cave.")* Once Saul went into a cave, not realizing that David and his men were hiding farther back in it. David quietly crept up on Saul and used his knife to cut off a piece of his robe as he was resting. But he would not let his men attack Saul. Later, when David was in a place where Saul couldn't get to him, he held up the piece of cloth to show Saul how he could have killed him if he had wanted to. Saul shed a few tears as if he were sorry for the way he had chased David, but it wasn't long before he was trying to kill him again.

(Take students to station 4.) One day, someone told Saul where David and his men were camped. Saul took 3,000 men to try to find David. That night when Saul and his men were sleeping David and a friend went into their camp. His friend encouraged David to kill Saul, but David refused. Instead, he took Saul's spear and water jug. The Lord had caused Saul and his army to fall into a deep sleep. David went some distance away and stood on a hill where Saul's army could see him. He shouted to Saul as he held up the spear and water jug. "Why are you trying to kill me?" David asked. "See? The Lord delivered you into my hands today, but I would not lay a hand on you." Finally, Saul went back home and quit chasing David. Not long after that, King Saul was badly wounded in a battle against the Philistines. Rather than let the enemy take him captive, he killed himself. David became king, not because of anything he had done to Saul, but because he had waited for the Lord to do His will.

Verse/Bulletin Board

Verse

"Be self-controlled and alert. Your enemy the devil prowls around like a roaring lion looking for someone to devour." (1 Peter 5:8)

How would David have reacted to Saul's threats if he hadn't been self-controlled? He would probably have killed him, which would have broken God's Law. David waited for God instead of trying to work things out on his own. For the Christian, self-control is actually Spirit-control because it is the Holy Spirit who gives us strength and control to put God first in our lives instead of our own selfish desires. Why doesn't the devil want us to be self-controlled? He has no power over us when we allow the Spirit to control us because God is much greater and strong than the devil.

Make 12–15 copies of the roaring lions pattern on page 24. Print the words and phrases of the memory verse on the lions. Lay them on a table in scrambled order. Challenge pairs of students to see how quickly they can put the words in order. Say the verse together after each attempt until students know it by heart.

Bulletin Board: "Practice Self-Control"

1. Cover the board with light green paper.

2. Print the caption and the two-line rhyme on the board as shown.

3. Brainstorm with students to come up with Bible verses and sayings about self-control. Print them on the board.

4. Let students look through magazines to find pictures and words that show some of the things the devil uses to tempt them to sin (money, wrong friends, anger, etc.). Have them cut these things out and mount them on the board around the words.

5. Talk about each thing mentioned or pictured on the board. How does the devil use this to tempt us to sin? How can we follow the Lord in this area instead of giving in to temptation?

6. Take a few minutes for group prayer. Encourage students to pray aloud, asking the Lord to give them self-control in every area of their lives.

Broken-Down Wall

Like a city whose walls are broken down

is a man who lacks self-control.

(Proverbs 25:28)

Directions: Read the verse above from Proverbs. How do you think a person without self-control is like a city with broken-down walls? Write your answer on the lines below.

_____

_____

Directions: Fit the words from the verse above into the crossword puzzle. The only word that does not go in the puzzle is "a."

Need Self-Control?

Directions: All of us could use more self-control. Where do you need to be more self-controlled? Look at the pictures. Do you have trouble in these areas of your life? Look up the Bible verses to find out what God wants. Match each verse to the correct picture. Write the verse reference at the bottom of each picture. Then on the back of this page, draw pictures of some other areas in which you need more self-control.

- Psalm 141:3
- 1 Corinthians 10:31
- Romans 12:2
- Ephesians 4:26
- Ecclesiastes 9:10

Too Late Now!

Directions: Before starting this object lesson, you will need a tube of toothpaste and a sheet of colored paper. Then tell the following story:

Have you ever said something and then wished you hadn't? Doesn't everybody at some time wish they could just keep their mouth shut? *(Hold up the opened tube of toothpaste.)* Let's let this tube of toothpaste represent our mouth. *(Call on a student to be your helper.)* Have you ever called someone a name that wasn't very nice? Maybe you thought it was funny, but the other person didn't think so. Let's squeeze out some toothpaste to stand for name calling. *(Give the toothpaste tube to the helper and have him or her squeeze out a dab of toothpaste on the colored paper.)* Have you ever told a lie? *(Have the helper squeeze out some toothpaste for a lie.)* Have you ever talked back to your parents or spoken disrespectfully to them? *(Squeeze out more toothpaste.)* Have you ever repeated a bad word you heard on TV? *(Squeeze out more toothpaste.)* Have you ever been rude or cross with someone? *(Squeeze out more toothpaste.)* Have you spoken God's name in a disrespectful way? *(Squeeze out more toothpaste.)* Have you said something about another person that was not true? *(Squeeze out more toothpaste.)*

Well, we have a lot of toothpaste on this paper, don't we? *(Hold up the paper so students can see it. Then speak to your helper.)* Ok, now take the toothpaste off the paper and put it back in the tube. *(Either your helper will immediately say that's impossible, or he or she will try and fail.)* You know what? The words we speak are like the toothpaste we squeezed out of this tube. They can't be taken back either! No matter how much you regret what you have said, once you've said it, it's too late to take it back. You can say you are sorry. You can slap your hand over your mouth. You can cry. But there is no way you can take it back any more than you can put toothpaste back in a tube once it is out.

And that is not just true for the words we speak, but also for anything we do. Once we tell a lie or lose our temper or look at something on TV that we should not or disobey our parents, it's too late to take it back. We cannot change it. We can only apologize and ask for forgiveness. That is why we need self-control. We need the Holy Spirit to stop us from doing wrong. It is so easy to say or do something without thinking, isn't it? But we can get into a lot of trouble that way and hurt other people, too. When we receive Jesus as our Savior, the Holy Spirit comes to live in us to guide us and help us in our everyday lives. He gives us self-control to help us think before we speak or act. If we pay attention to Him, we won't have to worry about taking anything back or being sorry for what we've done because we'll do the right thing to begin with.

The next time you brush your teeth, when you squeeze the toothpaste onto your toothbrush, remember how much you need to listen to the Holy Spirit and use the self-control He gives you.

"Teach me to do your will, for you are my God; may your good Spirit lead me on level ground." (Psalm 143:10)

Signs and Rhyme

Directions: Copy the sign patterns on pages 76–77 for children to color and cut out. Have them glue the signs to cardboard to make them sturdy, then to heavy cardboard strips for handles. Let them hold up the signs at the appropriate times as you say the rhyme together.

God gave us His Spirit
To give us self-control.
He helps and guides us every day
With signs to reach our goal.
STOP—GO—Take it SLOW!

When you start to tell a lie,
STOP! You know it's wrong.
GO ahead and tell the truth.
You knew it all along.
STOP—GO—Take it SLOW!

Don't make fun of anyone—
STOP before you start!
GO listen to the Spirit;
He's speaking to your heart.
STOP—GO—Take it SLOW!

When you want to go along
With that sinful crowd,
SLOW down and think about it,
Then STOP. Say no out loud!
STOP—GO—Take it SLOW!

If you always STOP and think
Before you speak or act,
The Holy Spirit's always there
to help you. That's a fact!
STOP—GO—Take it SLOW!

Sign patterns for activity on page 75.

Sign patterns for activity on page 75.

Fruit patterns for activity on page 78.

Culminating Activities

Fruit Basket Verses

Set a wicker basket on a table or attach it to a bulletin board. Enlarge the fruit patterns on page 77. Make two copies of each fruit. Color them and cut them out. Glue or staple them together to make two sided fruit, leaving the top open. Print the following Bible verse references on strips of paper to fit inside the fruits. Put the fruits in the basket. Encourage students to choose fruits and look up the Bible (NIV) verses before class begins or when they complete an assignment before the rest of the class.

Love—Matthew 5:44; Matthew 22:37–40; Romans 13:8–10; 1 Peter 2:17; 1 John 4:7

Joy—Psalm 70:4; Psalm 126:2–3; Romans 15:13; 1 Thessalonians 5:16; 1 Peter 1:8

Peace—Psalm 4:8; Isaiah 26:3; John 16:33; Romans 5:1; Colossians 3:15

Patience—Proverbs 15:18; 1 Corinthians 13:4; Ephesians 4:2; 1 Thessalonians 5:14; James 5:8

Kindness—Proverbs 14:21; Ephesians 4:32; Colossians 3:12; 1 Thessalonians 5:15; 2 Peter 1:5–7

Goodness—Psalm 34:14; Romans 12:9; Ephesians 5:8–10; Philippians 2:15; 1 Timothy 4:12

Faithfulness—1 Samuel 12:24; Proverbs 28:20; Ezekiel 18:9; Romans 12:12; 3 John 3

Gentleness—Proverbs 15:1; Ephesians 4:2; Philippians 4:5; 1 Peter 3:15

Self-Control—Proverbs 25:28; Romans 12:1–2; 1 Thessalonians 5:8; Titus 2:11–12; 1 Peter 5:8

Reward Badges

Make several copies of the fruit patterns on page 77. Print the word AWARD under the name on each fruit. Cover them, front and back, with clear adhesive plastic to make them durable. Buy pin backings in a craft shop or the craft area of a discount store. Glue a pin to the back of each fruit. When a student demonstrates the Fruit of the Spirit in your classroom, let him or her wear the award pin in class. Let the student wear the pin home to show the family that he or she is allowing the Holy Spirit to work in his or her life.

All the Fruit

Hold up a picture of an apple tree or draw one on the board. Ask students what kind of fruit they would expect to see growing on this tree. After they say that apples will grown on the tree, ask them what other kinds of fruit will grow with the apples. Could bananas grow on the same tree? Why not? What about grapes? Point out that a fruit tree only bears one kind of fruit, but God's Word promises that each Christian will bear all nine fruits of the Spirit. He does not give one person joy and another person love and somebody else patience. He gives each one of us all nine: love, joy, peace, patience, kindness, goodness, faithfulness, gentleness, and self-control. Of course, one person may show more love than someone else. Or I may have more self-control than you. But the Holy Spirit wants to help us develop every single one of these fruits in our lives. If someone saw an apple tree with several different kinds of fruit on it, do you think they would stare at it in amazement? If we allow the Holy Spirit to grow all His different fruits in our lives, people will be amazed. They will see that we are different, and they will want to know why.

Answer Key

Page 7

1. poured
2. forever
3. unfailing
4. everlasting
5. great
6. priceless
7. abounding
8. Son

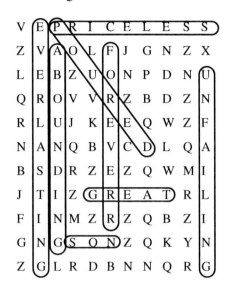

Page 8

JESUS LOVES YOU

Page 15

1. REFUGE
2. ETERNAL
3. JUBILANT
4. OVERFLOW
5. INMOST
6. COME
7. EXALTED

Page 19

HE WILL REJOICE OVER YOU WITH SINGING.

Page 25

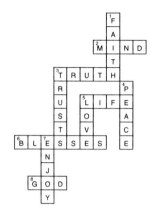

Page 26

2. Jesus
3. Underline "peace."
4. Underline twice "Do not let your hearts be troubled" and "do not be afraid."
5. "I have told you these things, so that in me you may have peace. In this world you will have trouble. But take heart! I have overcome the world."

Page 27

We have peace with God because Jesus died and rose again.

Page 37

A hot-tempered man stirs up dissension, but a patient man calms a quarrel.

Page 40

1. LITTLE KIDS
2. ENEMIES
3. ANIMALS
4. BUS DRIVER
5. CUSTODIAN
6. TEACHERS
7. PASTOR
8. STORE CLERKS

Page 41

Answers will vary.

Answer Key

Page 42

1. names
2. fun
3. listen
4. rude
5. words
6. helpful
7. Accept
8. down
9. unkind
10. you

Page 48

blameless, pure, and without fault

Page 49

1. darkness

2. light, Answers will vary.

3. as children of light, Answers will vary.

4. Read the Bible, pray, etc.

Page 56

1. all, promises
2. forever
3. never
4. generations
5. death, future, powers, anything

```
L  I  K  N (P) Z  Q  L  R  B
(F  U  T  U  R  E) S  N (G) G
S  B  N (F  O  R  E  V  E  R)
V  Q (N) R  M  Q  B  Z  N  J
J  L  E  M  I  D  Z  Y  E (P)
V  L  V (D) S  Z  Z  J  R  O
Y  W  E  Q  E  X  C  J  A  W
X  B  R  Z  S  A  V  V  T  E
(A) Y  B  J  Z  T  T  Z  I  R
W  L  Z  B  Q  J  Z  H  O  S
Q  R  L  R  B  C  P  S  N  D
(A  N  Y  T  H  I  N  G) S  G
```

Page 58

1. B   2. E   3. D   4. G   5. H

6. F   7. C   8. A

Page 60

The king saw four men in the furnace, the three men unharmed and a fourth man that looked like "a son of the gods." Shadrach, Meshach, and Abednego were not harmed at all. Their hair was not cinged, their robes were not scorched, and there was not even the smell of fire on them.

Page 65

Let your gentleness be evident to all. The Lord is near.

Page 66

1. give
2. heart
3. burdened
4. Take
5. humble
6. weary
7. learn
8. easy
9. rest
10. souls

Page 72

```
        ¹W  H  O      ²M
    ³I      A          A      ⁴B
  ⁵S  E  L  F  ⁶C  O  N  T  R  O  ⁷L
        L      I          O      I
  ⁸L  ⁹A  C  K  S      ¹⁰W      K      K
     R      T          H      E      E
     E          ¹¹D  O  W  N
                   S
                   E
```

Page 73

Anger–Ephesians 4:26

Food–I Corinthians 10:31

TV–Romans 12:2

Schoolwork–Ecclesiastes 9:10

Language–Psalm 141:3